A Little Motivation

This Book marks my 1 year anniversary on Keto Diet. I have lost 104 pounds and have gained a whole new outlook on food. I wanted to do something to honor the past year today, so I wrote a list of things that have helped me. I hope it can help you reading this with your own goals.

1. **Don't deprive yourself**. One reason I've done well on Keto is because nothing is off limits. In the past, I've had diets where I've had to cut something out, or I'd feel guilty when I indulged. Eventually, I'd get tired of saying no, and the diet wouldn't last.

2. **Life is about balance**: If I know I'm going to have an indulgent dinner, I'll eat a cleaner breakfast or lunch. It is ok to eat fast food, sweets, pasta, junk food, etc. But just learn to control yourself overtime

3. **Eat a lot of protein**: When I first started, I thought I would be hungry all the time, because I was limiting my food intake. To stay full, I had to get smarter about what I was putting in my body, and protein helps me fill full.

4. **Lean on your friends** It wasn't all strangers on the Internet who inspired me. Get yourself a friend like Ruth. She's someone I can talk to about mundane things, like what I ate for breakfast, but also more important things, like my biggest insecurities. Also, seeing my sister accomplish so much this past year has done wonders for me. It is empowering to see someone you know achieve the results you want.

5. **One meal won't make you fat**. I've had plenty of indulgent meals this past

year, but I've been consistently eating healthy meals and tracking everything I eat. A good meal every now and then won't hurt your weight loss journey; it'll just keep you sane.

6. **You can't ruin your diet**: The only thing that can ruin your diet is giving up completely. I've learned how to change my mindset so that if I get off track, I can always hit the restart button with the next meal. Don't wait until the next day or the next week to restart!

7. **Love what you eat**. One thing that has helped me stay on this journey is eating lighter versions of the foods I love. For example, I love Halo Top or Enlightened just as much as higher-calorie ice cream.

8. **Talk to yourself how you would talk to a friend**: Negative thoughts about how you look and what you've done or haven't done aren't going to

Measurement

I try to take my measurements around once a month. It can be a huge motivator to see how far I've come. I love holding out the measuring tape to see the dimensions of the old me. It seems unreal!

Arms: -3 inches

Waist: -11 inches

Hips: 12 inches

Thighs: -8 inches

Calf : -3 inches

If you're just starting your journey take your measurements! The scale isn't everything. I love looking at different sources to show me what I'm doing is working.

MAIN DISHES AND DINNER   76

APPETIZER — 216

HOW TO EXPLORE THIS BOOK

In the First part of the book the Ketogenic diet thoroughly explained for beginners, other diets including allergy-related diets were explained. Foods to eat and those to avoid for the different diet were listed out so that you can easily structure your diet to suit you.

Diet that was discussed includes; Paleo, dairy-free, gluten-free, Vegan, etc. In the second section, over 150 customable recipes were provided to keep you on your desired diet. For easier understanding, each recipe comes with the corresponding dietary option.

Dairy-Free

Gluten-Free

Nut-Free

Paleo

Vegan

AIP and so on

At the end of each recipe, you will find a breakdown of the calories, protein, fat, protein and net carbs per serving. This nutritional information is calculated from the recipe provide but please note that any changes you make to the ingredients will change the nutritional information.

To make things easier, I have created and index of all the allergies, all you need to do is visit the index, locate your allergy/Diet and get tons of Ketogenic recipes available for you.

INTRODUCTION

The Ketogenic Diet is on the rise not only for its efficiency in weight loss but also because it increases mental clarity, eliminate sugar, balances hormones and blood sugar level.

On the course of my different diets, I have personally noticed the difficulties people pass through trying to be faithful to a diet. We all have this problem of discovering the mix of diet that will be suitable for us, making us want to try them all. Can be puzzling right? Well we are all on a Confused Diet

It is at some point impossible not to cheat on a diet, either because of health setbacks or normal uncontrollable cravings.

Speaking of health, combining independent allergies while trying to lose weight can really be stressful. I am saying this out of experience, I come from a family with strong ancestral allergy, I have a high gluten sensitivity, Lactose/Dairy protein intolerance and diabetes. I so watch what I eat to the extent that I hardly eat out.

Hey!! Not to scare you, if you are in my shoes, here's a solution. I titled this cookbook "**Confused Keto**" because of the nature of recipes in it. The book is designed to help anyone and everyone that wants to lose weight. Whether you have keto as your main diet then other secondary diet to back it up, this works.

Be it **Lazy Keto, Clean Keto, Vegan, Dairy-free, Sugar-Free, Paleo, Gluten-Free, Nut-Free, Whole30, AIP, Natural Keto** and so on, this cookbook has been designed to be amenable to all expectation and dietary choice.

It contains over 150 recipes with nutritional information, the end point is that you will be eating right, shedding pounds and living your life.

The scrumptious recipes are classified in Appetizers, Desserts, Breakfast, Main Dishes and Side Dishes, very easy to make and will help you lose weight while nourishing your body

I'm the first one to admit that I love my fats. They are incredibly fueling and since I began to incorporate more fat into my breakfasts, I've personally experienced a huge improvement in health including weight loss, hormone balance and better sleep. You might be hearing a lot about high-fat diets since the ketogenic diet, or keto diet, has surged in popularity. And from where I stand, dropping the fear of fat and including nutritious sources of fat in our diets is a good thing.

What Is the Ketogenic Diet and How Does It Work?

The ketogenic diet is a low-carbohydrate, high-fat diet. It's kind of similar to other low-carb diets like Atkins, but instead of replacing carbs with protein, you add in a ton of fat. This sends the body into ketosis, where we start burning fat as our primary source of energy.

The ketogenic diet has actually been around for almost a century. It was initially developed in the 1920s to treat epilepsy and has since been used to help with weight loss, cardiovascular health, diabetes, brain disorders and certain types of cancer.

A Quick Review of Fats

Fat is an important macronutrient that has unfortunately been vilified for decades. Emerging research shows that all of the low-fat advice we grew up with was unfounded and fat doesn't lead to obesity and heart disease.

THE ROLE OF FAT IN THE BODY:

- Helps form our cell membranes
- Offers us a rich source of energy
- Protects our nervous system
- Helps us make hormones
- Forms our brains
- Supports effective functioning of the nervous system
- Nourishes our skin from the inside out
- Stabilizes blood sugar levels
- Lubricates our joints

All crucial stuff, right? So you can see why eliminating it could potentially cause us harm, while eating more of it can benefit our health and wellness.

How Did the Ketogenic (Keto) Diet Become Popular?

As I mentioned, the keto diet was initially used by doctors to treat epilepsy, particularly in children. The diet waned from the 1970s onwards (likely due to the belief that high fat diets were at the root of heart disease- a theory that has since been disproven). The diet was brought to the forefront again in 2000 when an episode of Dateline featured the story of a little boy suffering from epilepsy - and the medications weren't working. His seizures became so bad his parents turned to the ketogenic diet as a last resort and it cured him completely. (His parents went on to found a non-profit organization and direct a TV movie about their son that starred Merryl Streep.)

After that, scientists found a renewed interest in the ketogenic diet and began to explore it in more detail through clinical studies. What they found was substantial!

The Health Benefits of the Ketogenic Diet

The ketogenic diet has a wide range of crucial health benefits, including:

1. **Weight Loss:** Fat isn't going to make us fat. When we consume the right amount of fat for our bodies, we feel more satisfied and satiated. We don't ride on the blood sugar roller coaster. A number of singular studies (like this one) show that participants on ketogenic diets lose more weight than those on low-fat diets. And they keep it off - this meta-analysis concluded that high-fats diets were better than low-fat ones in the long run.

2. **Cardiovascular Disease:** The weight loss studies I referred to above also examined cardiovascular risk factors. The participants didn't experience negative cardio impacts from eating fat and the meta-analysis found that the keto diet helped to lower blood pressure and raise HDL cholesterol. Another meta-analysis that focused on the keto diet and heart health concluded that very low-carb diets help to lower blood

pressure and LDL cholesterol, raise HDL cholesterol, improve blood vessel function and reduce inflammation.

3. **Type 2 Diabetes Management + Blood Sugar Control:** Eating fat stabilizes our blood sugar levels. In one study comparing the keto diet to the low glycemic index diet, the keto diet group experienced a greater improvement in glycemic control and some participants were even able to reduce their diabetes medications. Other studies show that the keto diet, when compared to low-fat eating, can lower glucose and insulin concentrations and improve insulin sensitivity. In this study of Type 2 diabetes patients, most of the participants were able to eliminate or drastically reduce their meds.

4. **Epilepsy:** The keto diet is considered a valid option as part of treatment for epilepsy, though more so in children than adults. In this study of children with challenging seizures, the kids followed the keto diet for a year. Researchers followed up with the families three years and six years later, discovering that many of the children either decreased or eliminated their medications.

5. **Brain Health:** Our brains are about 60% fat. Emerging evidence indicates that ketone bodies can help improve memory and can potentially treat Alzheimer's disease.

Other areas of research indicate that ketogenic diets may be able to improve acne, symptoms of Parkinson's disease, suppress or reduce cancer tumors, diminish PCOS symptoms, and help heal brain trauma.

Is The Ketogenic Diet Right for You?

We are all biochemically unique, which is why I recommend people work with their favourite natural health care practitioner (this is mine) to ensure they are following a safe ketogenic diet, especially if you have metabolic conditions where medications are concerned.

If you are interested in experimenting with the ketogenic diet, try it for a couple of weeks and see if you notice a difference in your health. We all have different metabolic types, and some of us will feel better than others on a high-fat diet.

This may be stating the obvious, but it's virtually impossible to do this safely if you're vegan. There is only so many nuts, seeds and coconut you can eat, and you probably won't feel satiated or vibrant without the animal side of things. But if you've done it successfully, then let me know!

A ketogenic diet is a diet with so little carbohydrate in it that the body is forced to use fat (instead of sugar) as its primary fuel source. Clearly this has advantages for weight loss, but it apparently has other advantages as well. Since ketogenic diets are by definition high in fat (and moderate in protein), they don't jack blood sugar up, and therefore the demand on the body for insulin is greatly reduced. When insulin is no longer elevated all the time—the way it frequently is on a high-carb diet—the cells begin to regain their sensitivity to insulin and insulin resistance begins to fade. As everyone who reads my columns knows, insulin resistance is a factor in a baker's dozen of degenerative diseases, so anything that increases insulin sensitivity (reducing insulin resistance) is a pretty terrific thing for health and longevity.

Ketones—also known as ketone bodies—are produced as a by-product of fat-burning. And they are a terrific fuel for the heart, the muscles and the brain. And let's remember that cancer cells thrive on sugar—it's really their only fuel.

1. So when you reduce sugar in the diet (and the bloodstream), you're essentially depriving cancer cells of the fuel they need to survive and spread. Ketogenic diets are now being proposed as an adjunctive cancer therapy (

2. Anecdotally, some well-known people in the health and fitness space— namely superstar Hollywood trainer Vinnie Tortorich– have credited a ketogenic diet with keeping their cancer in remission. And noted researcher (and TED lecturer) Terry Wahls, M.D., has pioneered ketogenic diets for multiple sclerosis, plus she is currently conducting trials of her particular form of the diet—known as the Wahls protocol— for MS patients.

To summarize, the ketogenic diet is essentially "very low carbohydrate high fat diet" (abbreviated LCHF)—one that produces a state known as nutritional ketosis. People who follow keto diets usually monitor their ketone levels with devices that allow them to measure ketones in the blood, the urine, or, more recently, through the breath.

The Keto Foods and Grocery List

Ketogenic foods are foods which are low in carbohydrate, high in fat and lower in protein.

A general list of these foods includes both animal and plant based foods, but they are all real, whole foods such as:

- Meats, poultry and seafood in any form, preferably grass fed or wild caught (for instance, imitation crabmeat is not wild caught and has sugar and starch in it.) You can choose from beef, pork, chicken, turkey, shellfish, fish and the higher the fat content of the meat, the better. Dark meat thighs or better options than lean chicken breast, for example.
- Eggs, in any form. Deviled eggs make great snacks, and eggs in many forms are typically are a breakfast foundation food. Quiche, scrambled eggs, omelets, poached eggs, hard boiled eggs are all good choices.
- Natural Fats: I believe one should only eat real, organic fats like butter, cream and coconut oil, but if you want to include commercial mayonnaise, vegetable oils and olive oil, you can. However, I do advise leaning toward butter, olive oil and coconut oil, and limiting your intake of refined vegetable oils (soybean, canola, safflower, sunflower or corn oil) as they are high in Omega 6 fatty acids and can contribute to a long list of health issues associated with inflammation.
- Green leafy vegetables such as lettuce, spinach, kale, collards, cucumbers and high fiber cruciferous vegetables such as broccoli, cauliflower and cabbage. You'll need to track how much of the sweeter vegetables you eat (tomatoes, peppers, summer squash) because these are higher in carb. A whole plate of tomatoes will quickly put you over your carb limit.

This low carb food list of foods are also allowed on a ketogenic diet.

Cooking is a Big Part of Eating Well

As you look over these lists, you'll notice that these foods are close to their natural state. This means they require cooking to prepare them properly. This is an important point to remember.

Eating a healthy ketogenic diet means you'll need to spend more time in the kitchen. Most processed foods are convenient of course, but they are also full of sugar and starch.

If you are switching to a ketogenic foods diet for health reasons, giving up processed food and learning to cook for yourself are major steps on the path to better health.

However, If You Really Hate to Cook

If you don't know how to cook, and don't want to learn, there are ways to still eat ketogenic foods. There are lots of restaurants which have low carb options on the menus, and in a pinch, you can get a fast food hamburger and just avoid eating the bread.

There are restaurants which offer low carb choices, or gluten free menus which are usually lower in carb. The trick is to plan ahead. Usually, you can get the menu of a restaurant on the internet, then you'll have time to really look at it and make a wise choice without the pressure of the waiter or waitress waiting for your decision.

Your best bet for staying on plan is to order some sort of roasted or broiled meat and a salad with the dressing on the side. Or order a salad as a meal, such as a big Caesar with broiled chicken on top. Just be mindful of vinagrette dressings, they usually have a lot of sugar in them. Creamy dressings are usually higher in fat and lower in carb.

There are also grocery stores which offer pre-cooked foods such as roasted chickens, steamed shrimp, beef brisket, etc. Through in a salad with some full fat dressing and you have a keto meal.

However, I think that part of the journey toward better health is developing a habit of caring for yourself, and I can't think of a better way than to be able to make a delicious meal out of real, whole foods for yourself.

The Dairy Free Keto-
You May Have Lactose Intolerance and Not Even Realize It

Even if you don't think dairy is a problem for you, you may still have some form of lactose intolerance or dairy protein allergy. In fact, you may be struggling to break down lactose (milk sugar) without realizing it.

This is because, the majority of the human population — approximately 65 percent — has a reduced ability to digest lactose after infancy. More specifically, if you are of East Asian, West African, Arab, Jewish, Greek, and Italian descent, then you are highly likely to have some form of lactose intolerance.

Conversely, the prevalence of lactose intolerance is lowest in people with ancestors who depended on unfermented milk products as a primary food source. For this reason, only about 5 percent of people of Northern European descent are lactose intolerant.

In other words, if your ancestors didn't drink a lot of milk, then you probably have some form of lactose intolerance. This happens because our bodies stop producing the lactase enzyme that helps break down lactose (milk sugar) after being weaned off of breastfeeding.

Why does this happen?

Throughout our evolutionary history, we rarely encountered lactose unless it was from our mother's milk. Thus, our bodies produce lactase during our first years of life to help us digest the breastmilk and divert that energy elsewhere once we start eating solid food.)

Without the lactase enzyme, lactose is metabolized by gut bacteria, which can cause stomach upset, flatulence, diarrhea, bloating, nausea, and a host of familiar but unwelcome gastrointestinal symptoms. But don't worry, this isn't life threatening — it is just annoying and can make life difficult and unpleasant.

If you find that you feel worse after eating a dairy-heavy meal, then you may have some degree of lactose intolerance. To verify if you actually do struggle with lactose, you can get a breath test or a blood glucose test after drinking a lactose-rich drink, but these are much more time intensive and cost more money.

The simplest way to test for lactose intolerance is by mixing lactose powder with water and drinking it to see if digestive issues emerge. To do this, start with 25 grams of lactose first thing in the morning or 3 hours after your last meal. After drinking the lactose drink, pay attention to how you feel.

Take notice if one or more of these symptoms develop:

- abdominal cramps
- bloating
- diarrhea
- stomach or intestinal pain
- gassiness (burping or flatulence)
- indigestion

If one or more of these symptoms occur after drinking the lactose-drink, then you have some degree of lactose intolerance. The severity of the symptoms is a good indicator as to how well your body can handle lactose-containing foods.

For those who have minor symptoms during the lactose powder test, you can probably handle the amount of lactose you'll be getting with the ketogenic diet. On the other hand, if the lactose causes some serious digestive distress, here are some things that you can do:

- Limit your dairy intake and eat mostly low-lactose dairy products like hard cheese and butter.
- Take a lactase enzyme supplement right before eating dairy-heavy meals.
- Eliminate all dairy from your diet by following the recipes in this book

The good news is that the ketogenic diet tends to be much lower in lactose than any other dairy-containing diet, so you may only get minor side effects with some keto meals. However, if your body is struggling with low-lactose dairy products like butter or cheddar cheese, then you may have a dairy allergy or an intolerance to dairy protein, not lactose intolerance.

DAIRY ALLERGIES AND DAIRY PROTEIN INTOLERANCE

According to population-based studies, cow's milk allergy is the most common food allergy in infants and young children. As many as 2 in every 100 children under 4 years old are allergic to milk. Fortunately, dairy allergies are less prevalent among adults and older kids.

Dairy allergies commonly provoke immediate and unmistakable immune response. For example, you might get severely plugged sinuses, itchy skin, hives or rashes, diarrhea, nausea, vomiting, an elevated heart rate, and/or have difficulty breathing.

Dairy protein intolerances, on the other hand, are a bit more confusing and nuanced. Some of the symptoms are similar to and milder than those of allergic reactions. For some people, it can manifest as constipation or diarrhea.

For others, they will get joint pain or brain fog. Whatever the symptoms, they usually take longer to appear, making identification difficult. Plus, little scientific consensus exists on the nature of dairy protein intolerance. There are no universally accepted lab tests and few medical professionals will be able to help.

To make this concept of dairy allergy and intolerance easier to understand, think of them both as being on the same spectrum. All the way to the left of the spectrum, you have someone who has no problem with dairy proteins at all — they can them all day and have no issues.

As you move toward the right of the spectrum, you have an increasing level of intolerance that can cause mild intestinal discomfort to a minor allergic reaction, and all the way to the right side of the spectrum, you have someone who goes into anaphylaxis after a drop of milk hits their tongue.

Where you fall on this spectrum depends on your genetics, your gut health, your diet, your lifestyle, and your upbringing. Thus, some people may move to the left or the right of the dairy intolerances and allergy spectrum throughout life or on any given day. In fact, some people may even be able to eliminate the dairy intolerance completely with the right diet and lifestyle choices.

Whether you have some degree of lactose intolerance, dairy protein intolerance, or dairy allergy, it is up to you how much dairy you include in your diet. Obviously, if the consumption of lactose or dairy protein sends you into anaphylaxis or makes you feel absolutely dreadful, then you should convert to a dairy-free diet by **adhering strictly to the recipes listed in this book**. But what if you aren't sure?

I'd suggest figuring out if dairy is truly an issue for you. Although there are a couple of allergy tests that test for dairy allergies, they tend to be inaccurate. A much more telling method is following a dairy elimination diet. In other words, you must eliminate all dairy from your diet for about a month. By doing so, you will have the opportunity to notice if you feel better without dairy, and if you feel worse when you introduce it back into your diet.

How You Can Find Out If Dairy Should Be in Your Diet or Not

(Disregard if you are already certain of a dairy free diet)

By removing all dairy from your diet for around 30 days, you will give your body a break from any residual effects that dairy may be having on you. After going without dairy for this period of time, you will be ready start slowly reintroducing dairy back into your diet.

Begin by introducing casein-rich, low-lactose and whey foods back into your diet. This means dairy products like cheddar cheese, parmesan cheese, swiss cheese, and casein protein powder. After one day of eating these foods, assess how you feel. Do you feel better, worse, or the same?

Eliminate all dairy again for another 2-3 days, then introduce other dairy products like butter and heavy cream.

These contain both casein and whey, so you'll be testing if your body reacts negatively to whey protein (if it didn't react to casein with the earlier test). Assess how you feel after you have both whey and casein back in your diet. Do you feel better, worse, or the same?

Let another 2-3 days pass without dairy and test your lactose tolerance to other common keto foods. You can do this by having keto meals that contain half and half, heavy cream, sour cream, whole milk and/or cream cheese. How do you feel with this amount of lactose back in your diet? Better, worse, or the same?

If you feel worse when adding any of the dairy products back in, then take them out of your diet again to see if you feel better once again without them. On the other hand, if you feel better with less lactose in your diet, then consider keeping butter and natural aged low-lactose cheeses like cheddar, parmesan, and swiss in your diet and eliminating heavy cream, half and half, sour cream, and other keto dairy products with higher lactose content.

For those who fare poorly with low-lactose cheeses and most other dairy products, they will feel best when they remove all dairy from their diet. They should stick to eating dairy-free keto recipes and using the other dairy alternatives that we will go over later in the article.

Think of this dairy elimination diet as a brief experiment — a way to get in tune with your body and what will make you feel at your best in every way. This approach will require a lot of trial and error, but it is worth it if you want to optimize your health and well being for the rest of your life.

Many of us have some form of dairy intolerance, whether it is lactose intolerance, dairy protein intolerance, or a full blown milk allergy.

To find out if your body struggles with dairy here is what you can do:

lactose tolerance test

1. Mix 25 grams of lactose powder in water and drink it.
2. If you start getting the symptoms of lactose intolerance, then you probably struggle with digesting lactose-containing foods like heavy cream, half and half, sour cream, cream cheese, and whole milk.
3. Eliminate all dairy from your diet for at least a month. Do you feel better without dairy in your diet? Perhaps, your body was struggling with the lactose or dairy proteins.
4. After going dairy-free for a month, reintroduce dairy into your diet one dairy product at a time.
5. Start with hard cheeses like parmesan and cheddar. If you notice any negative symptoms emerge, then you are most likely intolerant to casein.
6. After 2-3 days of cutting out dairy again, reintroduce foods like butter and heavy cream. If you react to them, but not the hard cheeses, then you are probably intolerant to whey (this is very rare).
7. Depending on how you feel after doing these tests and how much you like dairy, it is up to you what you do with this information.

Here are some strategies for those who react negatively to dairy in some way:

1. Eliminate it from your keto diet entirely.
2. Reduce your dairy consumption to a point where you don't notice negative effects.
3. Take a lactase enzyme with your dairy-rich meal if you are only lactose intolerant.
4. Limit yourself to specific forms of dairy that you don't react to.

At this point, however, you may be wondering if it is even possible to be on a dairy-free ketogenic diet. After all, most of the recipes call for butter, heavy cream, or some form of cheese.

Yes, this is true, but it doesn't mean that you won't be able to eliminate all dairy from your diet. In fact, once you know what to avoid, what keto recipes to make, and what dairy alternatives you can use, you'll be able to live a dairy-free lifestyle just as easily as it is to live a dairy-filled lifestyle.

Things to avoid on Dairy Free Diet

Here is a comprehensive list of what you should avoid if you want to be completely dairy-free:

- Butter, butter fat, butter oil, butter acid, butter esters
- Buttermilk
- Casein, casein hydrolysate, rennet casein and caseinates (in all forms)
- Cheese (all animal milk based cheeses)
- Cottage cheese
- Heavy Cream
- Curds
- Custard and pudding
- Diacetyl
- Half-and-half
- Lactalbumin, lactalbumin phosphate, and lactoferrin
- Lactose, lactulose, and tagatose
- Milk (in all forms including condensed, derivative, dry, evaporated, goat's milk and milk from other animals, low-fat, malted, milk fat, non-fat, powder, protein, skimmed, solids, whole)
- Milk-based protein powders
- Sour cream, sour cream solids, and sour milk solids
- Whey (in all forms)
- Yogurt (in all forms)

Other possible sources of dairy proteins or lactose:

- Artificial butter flavor
- Baked goods
- Caramel candies
- Chocolate
- Lactic acid starter culture and other bacterial cultures
- Luncheon meat, hot dogs, and sausages that use the milk protein casein as a binder. Also, deli meat slicers are often used for both meat and cheese products, leading to dairy contamination.
- Margarine
- Nisin
- Non-dairy products that contain casein
- Nougat
- Shellfish may be dipped in milk to reduce the fishy odor. (Ask the seller if they do this when buying shellfish.)
- Brands of tuna fish that contain casein

- Some specialty products made with milk substitutes (e.g., soy, nut, or rice-based dairy alternatives) are manufactured on equipment shared with milk.
- Many restaurants put butter on grilled steaks to add extra flavor.
- Some medications contain milk protein.

Although not all of these products will contain lactose or milk proteins, it is important to be mindful of everything you are buying and eating. Make sure you read food labels carefully and ask questions if you're ever unsure about an item's ingredients.

Keep in mind, however, that while you are on the ketogenic diet, you will not encounter many of the ingredients/foods on the two lists above.

Foods to eat on Dairy Free Keto Diet

Now that you know what to avoid on the dairy-free keto diet, here is what you can eat:

1. Animal fats and plant-based oils. Avoid all fats that are derived from dairy and stick with plant-based oils like coconut oil, MCT oil, and olive oil and animal fats like lard, tallow, and duck fat.
2. Red meat, poultry, and seafood. Try to stick with organic, pasture-raised, and 100% grass-fed meat and wild caught fish where possible.
3. Low-carb vegetables. Stick with above ground vegetables, leaning toward leafy/green produce. Check out our low-carb vegetable guide to find out exactly what vegetables to eat on keto and how many carbs are in each one.
4. Low-carb fruits. Although most fruits are not keto-friendly, there are a handful that make a great addition to the ketogenic diet. Some examples of keto-friendly fruits are avocados, berries, and some citrus fruits. For a more detailed guide on what fruits you should and shouldn't eat on keto, click here.
5. Nuts and seeds. Eat nuts and seeds in moderation as some contain a decent amount of carbs. Try to use fattier nuts like macadamias, pecans, and almonds.
6. Dairy alternatives. There are plenty dairy alternatives that you can use to replace common keto foods like heavy cream, cheese, sour cream, half and half, and yogurt.

The easiest way to cut dairy products out of your diet is by looking for dairy-free keto recipes and making a shopping list based on the ingredients. This way you will know for sure that you won't end up buying any products that contain dairy, while simultaneously ensuring that you will have plenty of delicious keto-friendly food to eat.

Once you get the hang of dairy-free shopping and cooking, feel free to experiment with different dairy substitutions to make your favorite dairy-heavy keto recipes into 100% dairy-free meals.

How to Implement the Dairy-Free Ketogenic Diet Meal Plan Properly?

With this dairy-free ketogenic meal plan template, you'll be able to map out what you need to get from the grocery store for a week's worth of meals while guaranteeing that you won't be consuming any dairy products at all.

I also tried to put together the meal plan so that you only have to make each recipe once a week and eat the leftover servings a couple of days later. This way, you can save time and money while you implement the dairy-free ketogenic diet.

Although I suggest how many servings you should eat, this doesn't mean that they will meet your specific calorie and macronutrient needs. Make sure you use the calorie breakdowns on the meals to guide your decision of how much to eat. Your meals should be big enough to meet your calorie, protein, and fat needs for the day without needing any snacks or dessert.

What do you do if you there are one or two dairy ingredients in your favorite keto recipe?

Use a dairy alternative.

Here are keto-friendly dairy alternatives for the most common dairy products that you will encounter on the ketogenic diet. Below the graphic, you'll find more detailed explanations on each substitution.

Common dairy substitutions on a ketogenic diet.

HOW TO REPLACE WHOLE MILK

The most reliable whole milk alternative is coconut milk. In recipes, you can substitute coconut milk in for regular whole milk in a 1 to 1 ratio.

However, make sure the coconut milk you are getting doesn't have any added sugar or carbs.

If the recipe calls for a lower fat milk, then use light coconut milk. Conversely, when the recipe calls for whole milk, use the richest coconut milk you can find (I prefer Aroy-d 100% Coconut Milk).

DAIRY-FREE HEAVY CREAM SUBSTITUTIONS

There are three effective heavy cream alternatives that I know of:

- Coconut Cream. You can either allow a can of full-fat coconut milk to settle (about 1/2 hour) and scoop the cream off the top or purchase coconut cream online or from the store. To substitute cream in recipes, use equal parts coconut cream for the dairy cream. This will work particularly well in sauces for seafood and poultry.
- High-Protein Soy Cream Alternative. Blend Silken Tofu until smooth. This pureed tofu can be substituted for heavy cream using a 1:1 ratio. It works as an excellent cream substitute when a thickener is needed in sauces and soups. Choose medium firm or firm varieties for a thicker "cream".
- Milk + Oil Heavy Cream Replacement. Blend 2/3 cup of soy or rice milk with 1/3 cup of oil (extra light olive oil is best for cooking). This will replace 1 cup of heavy cream for your recipes. Keep in mind, however, that it will not whip.

How to Replace Sour Cream

- Although these don't taste exactly like sour cream, they do the trick:
- Vegan Yogurt. Use a plain unflavored and unsweetened variety of dairy-free yogurt as a 1:1 sour cream substitute. Works best in dips and salad dressings.
- Soy Sour Cream. Blend up some firm Silken Tofu for a wonderful sour cream like consistency. Use as a 1:1 sour cream substitute for more savory dishes.
- Nut-based Sour Cream. For a delicious soy-free sour cream alternative, you can make your own sour cream using cashews or sunflower seeds as the base. Google search "cashew sour cream" to find a recipe that works for you.

DAIRY-FREE BUTTER ALTERNATIVES

- For frying, use coconut oil, olive oil, or ghee (a butter product that has all of the dairy proteins taken out).
- For a buttery spread (for keto breads or muffins), use coconut butter, nut butter, or seed butter.
- For baking, use coconut butter (or coconut manna), a vegan butter (that doesn't contain hydrogenated oils), or ghee in the same way that you would use butter.
- You can also use olive oil for baking as well. If a recipe calls for 1/2 cup butter, try using 1/3 cup oil instead (this may require a bit of experimentation).

PALEO KETO DIET

The paleo keto diet is based on animal fat and protein consumption. It combines aspects of the paleo diet, which emulates the foods of our ancestors, and the

The focus is on eating nutritious, natural foods with much of the energy coming from animal products. Grains (bread, cereals) milk and other dairy products, vegetable oils, nightshades, refined sugars and processed foods are avoided.

Only a handful of case studies exist where experience with the paleo keto diet has been published. The diet has been tested as a means of treating type 1 and type 2 diabetes and has shown significant potential.

Subjects have been instructed to eat a fat: protein ratio of around 2:1. Animal meat, fat, offal, and eggs make up the core of the diet. Vegetables and fruit are eaten too, but to a lesser extent. A small amount of honey might be allowed for sweetening.

Energy balance

The paleo keto diet provides more energy compared to a diet high in starchy carbohydrates, and also enables a more balanced supply of energy.

Carbohydrate

Patients are advised not to eat more than 30 grams of carbs per day initially. Lower plant food intake is recommended, while food can be sweetened with honey.

Protein

Fatty and red meats are encouraged over lean meats. Patients often eat beef steak, fried bacon and roasted ribs as core meals. Offal, such as bone marrow, liver and kidney, is advised to help maintain healthy vitamin levels.

Eggs are also recommended as part of meals.

Fat

Meats can be cooked and eaten with fried lard to ensure a fat: protein ratio of around 2:1 in grams. An adequate ratio of protein to fat is important; eating too much protein can prevent the development of ketosis.

Grocery List for Diary and Gluten-Free Diet

Veggies:

All Greens like: Parsley, Cilantro, Broccoli, Bok Choy, Spinach, Green lettuce, Cabbage (Green or Red), Celery, Fresh Dill, Avocados, Brussels sprouts, Bean Sprouts, Asparagus, Snow Peas, Cucumber, Cauliflower, Zucchinis, Fresh green onions, Yellow or Red Raw onions.

Ferments:

Fermented Sauerkraut, Fermented Gut Shots, Fermented Kimchi

Poultry: (Organic and Grass Fed if you can)

- Chicken Thighs, Wings, Legs, Grounded Chicken, Chicken Bone Broth
- Turkey Legs, Grounded Turkey, Turkey Breast, Whole Turkey, Turkey Bacon (Nitrate free), Turkey Sausage.

Beef of all kinds (make sure that they are Grass Fed), Roast beef, Baby Back Ribs, Steak all cuts and Beef Bone Broths

Pork: Bacon (Nitrate free), Pork chops, Tenderloin, Ground Pork, Pork Roast, Ham (unglazed)

Seafood: Bass, Cod, Salmon, Haddock, Halibut, Shrimp, Sole, Trout (Make sure that the seafood you eat is WILD) *Never eat Farmed Fish avoid at all cost*

Sauce: Apple cider vinegar, Yellow or brown mustard, Lakanto Maple syrup (Keto Friendly), Lemon juice, Lime juice, Ranch (my homemade Hemp ranch dressing, recipe under files), Sugar free Ketchup, Low carb Salsa.

Liquids: (Nondairy) Hemp milk, Coconut milk, Almond milk, Herbal Tea, Herbal Teas like (Dandelion, Green Tea, Chamomile, Pau D'Arcy), Coffee (Organic), Protein Powders from (Sun Warrior, Perfect Keto, Equip Food)

Spices: Paprika, Garlic powder, Oregano, Onion powder, Pink Himalayan Salt, Turmeric, Allspice, Chili powder, Cumin, Cinnamon ((Black pepper does contain carbs)) ---(Make sure your spice rack is Organic)

Fruits: Blackberries, Blueberries, Raspberries, Strawberries, Olives (Organic Greek Olives green or black)

Fats and Oils: Vegan / Soy Free Butter by: Earth Balance, Bacon Fat, Coconut oil, MCT Oil or the Powder by: Perfect Keto, Duck Fat / Lard, Mayo Vegan, Olive oil, Avocado Oil, Beef bone broth/Chicken bone broth, Coconut Cream.

Cooking and Baking: Coconut Flour, Almond Flour, Coconut Flakes, Coconut Meat, Coconut Water, Flax Meal, Flax seeds, Chia seeds, Cocoa powder, Nutritional Yeast, Macadamia Nuts, Brazilian Nuts, Cacao Nibs, Pistachios, Pumpkin Seeds, All Seeds.

Sweeteners: Erythritol, Stevia drops, Stevia Powder, Stevia Flavors, Vanilla Extract (any extracts are fine depending on your sweet tooth)

Keto VS Vegan

You may be wondering what plant-based foods are keto-friendly and if it's possible to be vegan on a keto diet.

While there are certainly vegan items that should be avoided or limited—like starchy root vegetables, beans, and berries—there are tons of healthful, satisfying vegan foods, from leafy greens and cauliflower to almond butter and tofu, that you can eat when trying a keto diet!

Remember, plant-based diets are clinically proven to be one of the best ways to lose weight and safeguard against obesity. While the keto diet may be fine to try for a short period of time, it's not recommended long term.

Additionally, scientific evidence that a nutritious plant-based diet is beneficial for your health continues to mount; countless studies show that vegans have lower rates of heart disease and diabetes and may even live longer!

And a vegan diet is a win-win situation: You get to live a longer, healthier life while letting farmed animals live their lives

BREAKFAST AND DESSERTS

Tofu in Purgatory (Shakshuka)

Dairy-Free, Gluten-Free, Sugar-Free, Nut-Free, Vegan

Prep Time: 5 Mins || Cook Time: 20 Mins

Breakfast, Brunch, Entree, Lunch

Servings: 2

Calories: 284 Kcal

Silky, soft tofu rounds cooked gently in a fiery, garlicky and chunky tomato sauce. Tofu in Purgatory is the perfect brunch dish!

Ingredients

- 1 tablespoon olive oil (optional)
- 4 large cloves of garlic
- 1 796 ml can diced tomatoes
- Salt & pepper to taste I used 1 teaspoon salt & ½ teaspoon pepper
- 2 teaspoons dried herbs see recipe note
- 1/2 teaspoon dried chili flakes use less if you prefer less heat
- 1 teaspoon sugar optional but helps to bring out the tomato flavor
- 1 block of unpressed medium tofu cut into rounds (around 350g although this doesn't have to be exact) see recipe note
- Indian Black Salt (Kala Namak) optional

Instructions

1. Warm the olive oil in a skillet and cook the garlic over medium heat until just starting to turn a little brown. (use a drop of water instead of the oil to keep the recipe oil-free).
2. Add the tomatoes, salt, pepper, chili flakes, herbs and optional sugar.
3. Simmer over a medium heat for 5 minutes then add the tofu rounds.
4. Turn down the heat to medium-low and simmer for 15 minutes until the sauce is thickening up a little and the tofu is soft and heated through.
5. Sprinkle the tofu with a little Indian Black Salt just before serving if you would like an eggy flavour.
6. Serve with toast, crusty bread or baguette to mop up the juice!

NOTES

Mixed herbs are good. I used Herbs De Provence but Italian Seasoning, oregano or rosemary would all be fine - Just use what you have.

Medium tofu is great for this recipe as once poached in the sauce it has a texture similar to poached egg white. I used a large block, cut it into ½ inch thick slices, then used a cookie cutter to cut the rounds. You don't have to make them round if you don't want to. It will taste the same no matter what the shape! Just keep the thickness to around ½ inch. Save your tofu off cuts to add to another meal. I used mine in a tofu scramble the next day. They keep in the freezer well if you won't be needing them for a while.

Serving: 1serving

Calories: 284kcal, Carbohydrates: 26.6g, Protein: 20.3g, Fat: 9.4g, Sodium: 983.6mg, Fiber: 9.2g, Vitamin A: 1450IU, Vitamin C: 71mg, Calcium: 370mg, Iron: 5mg

Keto coconut bread

Dairy-Free, Gluten-Free, Nut-Free

Cook Time: 50 Mins // Prep Time: 10 Mins

Makes: 16 Slices

Keto coconut bread is a fantastic substitute for my regular keto bread but it is nut free, gluten free and slightly lower in calories. The bread is fluffy, sliceable and totally delicious. Just make sure you keep some for yourself, because everyone will want a slice of the action.

Course Breakfast, Lunch, Snack

Ingredients

- 7 Large Eggs
- 1/2 cup Coconut Flour 40g / 1.2 oz.
- 1/2 cup olive/coconut oil
- 1/4 tsp. Salt
- 1/4 tsp. baking powder (aluminum free if possible)
- 1/2 tsp. xanthan gum (optional)

Instructions

1. Preheat oven to 180 C (355 F).
2. Crack the eggs into a bowl and mix for 1 minute until well combined.
3. Add the coconut flour, coconut oil, salt, baking powder and xanthan gum, and mix until completely combined. The mixture will become quite thick.
4. Line an 8.5 X 5-inch (21.5 x 12.7 cm) loaf tin with parchment paper and pour the batter into the tin. Level the top with a spatula if uneven.
5. Bake for 50 minutes or until a skewer comes out of the middle clean.
6. Nutrition information is for 1 slice. Slice and store in the fridge for up to 5 days or in the freezer for up to 2 weeks. This bread freezes well.

Calories 95 Calories from Fat 81, Total Fat 9g 14%, Saturated Fat 5g 25%, Cholesterol 97mg 32%, Sodium 117mg 5%, Potassium 32mg 1%, Total Carbohydrates 1g 0%, Dietary Fiber 1g 4%, Sugars 0.2g, Protein 3g 6%, Vitamin A 6%, Calcium 1%, Iron 4%

Sweet low carb Chocolate Keto Muffins

Gluten-Free, Nut-Free,

Per Serving: 215 calories, 1 net carb.

Servings: 12

This recipe uses healthy (estrogen balancing) flax seed instead of flour, making your muffins nut and Gluten-Free.

Ingredients:

- 2 c flax seed, ground
- 1 tbsp. baking powder
- 2 tsp. ground cinnamon
- 3 tbsp. unsweetened cocoa powder
- 1/2 tsp. salt
- 5 eggs, large
- 1/2 c filtered water, room temp
- 1/3 c melted coconut oil (or MCT oil)
- 2 tsp. vanilla extract
- 20-30 drops liquid stevia (sub chocolate stevia or 1/4 cup erythritol)

Instructions

1. Preheat oven to 350 F. Grease or line muffin tins/molds, and set aside.
2. Whisk together: flax seed, baking powder, cinnamon, cocoa powder and salt in a large bowl. Combine fully and set aside.
3. Using a high-powered (or hand-held) blender, mix together eggs, water, coconut oil (or MCT oil), vanilla and stevia. Blend at high speed 30 seconds, or until foamy.
4. Pour blended liquid mixture into the flax seed dry mix bowl. Stir with a spatula until lightly incorporated. Batter will be very fluffy. Let batter rest 3 minutes.
5. Spoon batter into muffin cups, about 90% of the way up. Muffins expand while baking.
6. Bake 13 to 15 minutes, or until an inserted toothpick/fork comes out clean.
7. When done, remove muffins from the cups immediately and place on a cooling rack.
8. Store muffins in the fridge up to 4 days, or freeze up to 3 months.

Per Serving: 215 Calories; 17g Fat (69.5% calories from fat); 8g Protein; 9g Carbohydrate; 8g Dietary Fiber.

Keto Sausage Frittata

Dairy-Free, Gluten-Free, Nut-Free

Serves: 4

Prep Time: 10 mins || Cook Time: 30 min

Cooking Type: Baking

Course: Breakfast

Serving Size: 1/8th frittata

Our keto frittata recipe is not just low-carb but due to the eggs which are a low-carb superfood. It's full of healthy fats, protein, and an unrivaled amino acid profile, truly the perfect low-carb keto breakfast. Keto Sausage Frittata – You must try this recipe.

Ingredients

-
- 2 tablespoons capers, drained
- 1/4 cup chopped sun-dried tomatoes
- 8 large eggs
- 1/4 cup water
- 1/2 teaspoon kosher salt
- 1/4 teaspoon ground black pepper
- 2 tablespoons chopped fresh basil, plus more for garnish if desired

Instructions

1. Preheat the oven to 375 degrees Fahrenheit.
2. Cook the sausage in a 10-inch oven proof skillet (see notes) over medium heat for 5 minutes, stirring to break into small pieces.
3. Add the capers and sun-dried tomatoes, cook for an additional 2 minutes.
4. Beat the eggs, water, salt, pepper and basil together in a large bowl.
5. Pour the egg mixture over the sausage mixture.
6. Bake for 25 minutes, or until firm.
7. Remove and cool slightly before cutting and serving with additional chopped basil if desired.

If you don't have an oven proof skillet, you can cook the sausage, capers and tomatoes in a regular skillet and then add them to an oven proof baking dish along with the egg mixture – and then bake as directed.

Calories: 220, Fat: 17g, Carbohydrates: 2g, Fiber: 0g, Protein: 15g

Egg Salad

Serves: 8

Prep Time: 5 mins ||

Course: Breakfast

This egg salad is healthy and so easy to make. It's a classic recipe with an addicting crunch from the delicious bacon.

Ingredients

- hard boiled eggs*
- 1/4 cup red onion diced
- 8 slices sugar free bacon cooked and crumbled
- 3/4 cup paleo mayonnaise or more to taste
- 1 tbsp dijon mustard
- 2 tbsp fresh chives thinly sliced
- 1/2 tsp sea salt or more to taste
- 1/4 tsp ground black pepper
- 1/4 tsp smoked paprika

Instructions

1. Peel the eggs and chop into small pieces. Place in a large bowl.
2. Add the rest of the ingredients to the bowl.
3. Use a spoon to stir together until combined.
4. Taste to adjust creaminess and seasoning with more Paleo mayo or salt.
5. Refrigerate for at least 2 hours before serving.

Calories 332 Calories from Fat 270

Total Fat 30g 46%, Saturated Fat 7g 35%, Cholesterol 268mg 89%, Sodium 539mg 22%, Potassium 141mg 4%, Total Carbohydrates 1g 0%, Protein 11g 22%, Vitamin A 8.8%, Vitamin C 1%, Calcium 3.9%, Iron 7.3%

*My favorite method for hard boiling eggs is in the Instant Pot.

- Pour 1 cup of water in, place a steamer rack in the pot, and add the eggs.
- Cook on manual pressure on High for 5 minutes. Let it release naturally pressure for 5 minutes. Place in an ice bath for at least 5 minutes, before peeling.

Easy Hard Boiled Eggs

Ever since I got the Instant Pot, it's the only thing I use to make hard boiled eggs because it's easy, quick, and they come out perfect and easy-to-peel every time. Don't have one? No worries. Here are both stove top and Instant Pot methods to make hard boiled eggs for this Whole30 egg salad:

Stove Top Method

1. Bring water to a boil in a saucepan.
2. Take out eggs straight from the fridge, then lower the eggs into the water so they don't break, and let it come to a boil again. Once it does, lower the heat, and let the eggs simmer for 11 minutes.
3. Prepare a large bowl with an ice bath.
4. Once the eggs are done cooking, place them in the ice bath for at least 15 minutes.
5. Peel the eggs under cold running water.

Instant Pot Method

1. Pour 1 cup of water into the Instant Pot, and place a steamer basket or the trivet it came with over the water.
2. Place the eggs on the steamer basket or the trivet.
3. Close the lid, and make the sure the pressure valve is set to Sealing.
4. Cook on high on Manual for 5 minutes, and prepare an ice bath.
5. Once it beeps to a finish, naturally depressurize for 5 minutes, then release the pressure.
6. Immediately transfer the eggs to the ice bath and let it sit for at least 5 minutes.
7. Peel the eggs. They should be peel easily!

Breakfast Sausage

Dairy-Free, Gluten-Free, Nut-Free

Serves: 12

Prep Time: 10 mins || Cook Time: 15 min

Cooking Type: Baking

Course: Breakfast

Breakfast Sausage - clean eating is simple with this easy homemade breakfast sausage recipe. Great for freezing too!

Ingredients

- 1 lb ground turkey (or pork or chicken)
- 1 teaspoon Italian seasoning see
- 1 teaspoon sage
- 1/2 teaspoon all-purpose salt free blend
- 1/2 teaspoon sea salt
- cooking oil of choice

Instructions

1. Combine ground turkey and seasonings in a bowl. Mix well with your hands and form 12 patties.
2. Heat a large skillet over medium heat. Add cooking oil (avocado, coconut, or olive oil) or ghee to the pan. Add patties to the pan (in batches) and cook 3-4 minutes per side, until nicely browned and cooked through.
3. Remove from pan and drain on paper towels if desired. Serve immediately, refrigerate, or freeze for future use.
4. Alternative to patties, make ground sausage by cooking ground turkey and spices together in the oil, breaking up into pieces.

Calories: 68kcal | Protein: 7g | Fat: 4g | Saturated Fat: 1g | Cholesterol: 31mg | Sodium: 123mg | Potassium: 80mg | Vitamin A: 30IU | Calcium: 11mg | Iron: 0.5mg

8-Ingredient Zucchini Lasagna (GF)

Dairy-Free, Gluten-Free, Sugar-Free, Vegan

Healthy, 8-ingredient lasagna made with zucchini noodles, organic red sauce, and macadamia nut ricotta "cheese"! Hearty, wholesome, and so delicious.

Prep Time: 20 Minutes || Cook Time: 1 Hour

Servings: 9 (squares)

Freezer Friendly: 1 month

Ingredients

VEGAN RICOTTA

- 3 cups raw macadamia nuts or soaked blanched almonds* (or 1 16-ounce block extra firm tofu*, drained and pressed dry for 10 minutes)
- 2 Tbsp nutritional yeast
- 1/2 cup fresh basil (finely chopped)
- 2 tsp dried oregano
- 1 medium lemon, juiced (~2 Tbsp or 30 ml as original recipe is written)
- 1 Tbsp extra virgin olive oil (optional // for flavor + richness)
- 1 tsp sea salt + pinch black pepper
- 1/2 cup water (plus more as needed // reduce if using tofu as it requires less)

THE REST

- 1 28-ounce jar favorite marinara sauce (I like Trader Joe's organic tomato basil)
- 3 medium zucchini squash thinly sliced with a mandolin (or sub eggplant with this recipe as a guide)

Instructions

1. Preheat oven to 375 degrees F (176 C).
2. Add macadamia nuts to a food processor or blender and mix to combine, scraping down sides as needed. You're looking for a fine meal.
3. Add remaining ingredients: Nutritional yeast, fresh basil, oregano, lemon juice, olive oil (optional), salt, pepper and water. You are looking for a well-puréed mixture/paste.
4. Taste and adjust seasonings as needed, adding more salt and pepper for flavor, nutritional yeast for cheesiness, and lemon juice for brightness.
5. Pour about 1 cup (amount as original recipe is written // adjust if altering batch size) marinara sauce into a 9×13-inch (or similar size) baking dish and line with thinly sliced zucchini.

6. Scoop small spoonfuls amounts of ricotta mixture over the zucchini and gently spread into a thin layer.
7. Spread on a layer of marinara sauce and then top with more zucchini slices. Continue until all filling and zucchini are used up. The top two layers should be zucchini and then sauce. Sprinkle on vegan parmesan cheese (optional), and then cover with foil.
8. Bake covered for 45 minutes, then remove foil and bake for 15 minutes more. The zucchini should be very easily pierced when cut with a knife. Let cool for 10-15 minutes before serving.
9. Serve immediately with additional vegan parmesan cheese and fresh basil. Leftovers keep for 2-3 days in the refrigerator, or in the freezer up to 1 month.

Notes

*If subbing blanched almonds, soak in cold water overnight (or 6 hours), or in very hot water 1 hour. Then drain thoroughly and proceed with recipe as written.

*If subbing tofu, make sure it's firm (not silken). Adjust seasonings as needed as the tofu requires a little bit more nutritional yeast, salt and basil.

*Nutrition information is a rough estimate calculated without vegan parmesan cheese or olive oil.

Nutrition (1 of 9 servings)

Serving: 1 squares

Calories: 395, Carbohydrates: 19g, Protein: 6.8g, Fat: 35.9g, Saturated Fat: 5.7g, Polyunsaturated Fat: 1.73g, Monounsaturated Fat: 26.7g, Trans Fat: 0g, Cholesterol: 0mg, Sodium: 585 mg, Potassium: 692mg, Fiber: 6.7g, Sugar: 10.6g, Vitamin A: 908 IU, Vitamin C: 24.97 mg, Calcium: 78.4 mg, Iron: 3.02 mg

Southwest Salmon Cakes with Avocado Ranch Aioli

Dairy-Free, Gluten-Free, Nut-Free

Prep Time: 5 Mins // Cook Time: 25 Mins

Yield: 8

Recipe Type: Breakfast

A simple salmon cake recipe with a southwest twist and the yummiest aioli sauce for dipping! These salmon cakes are paleo, and Keto!

Ingredients

- Salmon Cakes
- 4 6 oz cans boneless/skinless salmon, drained I like Wild Planet brand!
- 1/2 medium red onion diced
- 1/8 cup chopped fresh cilantro can use parsley if you prefer!
- 1 tbsp coconut aminos
- 1 tbsp dijon mustard
- 1/2 cup mayo
- 2 eggs
- 1/3 cup almond flour
- 1 tsp sea salt
- 1 tsp cumin
- 1 tsp chili powder

- 1 tsp garlic powder
- 1/2 tsp paprika
- 1 tbsp ghee or olive oil

Avocado Ranch Aioli

- 1 large avocado peeled and pitted
- 1/3 cup mayo
- 1 tbsp fresh lemon juice
- 2 cloves minced garlic
- 1/4 tsp sea salt
- 1/2 tsp dried parsley
- 1/2 tsp dried minced onion
- 1/2 tsp dried dill
- 1/2 tsp dried chives
- 2 tbsp water more if you want it thinner

Instructions

1. Preheat oven to 425. Combine all salmon cake ingredients in a large bowl and mix well, making sure to break up all of the salmon pieces.
2. Line a baking sheet with parchment paper. Use a pastry brush to spread cooking oil of choice over the parchment paper.
3. Use a 1/3 cup measuring cup to scoop up the mixture and form 8 1-inch thick patties using your hands. Place them on the baking sheet.
4. Bake for 15 mins, then remove from the oven and flip using a spatula. Return them to the oven for an additional 10 minutes until browned and cooked through.
5. While the cakes are baking, make the aioli. Combine all aioli ingredients in a blender and blend on high for 30 seconds. Add water as needed until desired consistency is reached.
6. Serve the salmon cakes with the aioli. Enjoy!

Avocado, Bacon and Balsamic

Dairy-Free, Gluten-Free, Nut-Free

Serves: 2

Prep Time: 5 mins || Cook Time: 5 min

Cooking Type: Cooking

Course: Breakfast

Perfect for a snack, or even breakfast.

Ingredients

- 1 avocado
- slices cooked bacon chopped
- 1 teaspoon aged balsamic vinegar to taste
- sea salt to taste

Instructions

1. Halve the avocado and remove pit.
2. Sprinkle with bacon, balsamic vinegar, and sea salt to taste.
3. Serve with a spoon.

Calories: 254kcal | Carbohydrates: 9g | Protein: 4g | Fat: 23g | Saturated Fat: 5g | Cholesterol: 14mg | Sodium: 153mg | Potassium: 530mg | Fiber: 6g | Sugar: 1g | Vitamin A: 145IU | Vitamin C: 10.1mg | Calcium: 12mg | Iron: 0.6mg

Pizza Breakfast Casserole

Dairy-Free, Gluten-Free, Nut-Free

Prep Time: 10 Mins // Cook Time: 35 Mins

Yield: 8

Recipe Type: Breakfast

An easy make-ahead breakfast bake with all the Italian flavors of your favorite pizza!

Ingredients

- 2 tbsp olive oil
- 12 eggs
- 2 tsp Italian seasoning
- 1 tsp sea salt
- 1/2 onion diced
- 1 green pepper diced
- 1 red pepper diced
- 1 lb Ground Italian or Breakfast Sausage if not using turkey sausage, sugar and nitrate free brand
- 10-12 regular or turkey pepperoni, sugar and nitrate free brand
- 1 14.5 can diced tomatoes drained

Turkey Sausage

- 1 lb lean ground turkey
- 1 tsp fennel seed
- 1 tsp salt
- 2 tsp sage
- 1 tsp thyme
- 1 tsp black pepper
- 1/2 tsp cayenne
- 1/2 tsp garlic powder

Instructions

1. Preheat oven to 350. Spray a 9x13 inch casserole dish with olive oil or avocado oil.
2. Make sausage. Heat a large sauté pan over medium high heat and add 1 tbsp olive oil. If making turkey sausage, add all ingredients and cook 5-7 minutes until no longer pink.
3. If using other sausage, cook 5-7 minutes until browned and cooked through.

4. Add cooked sausage to the bottom of the casserole dish. Using the same pan, add remaining olive oil and chopped onions and peppers.
5. Cook until onion is opaque and beginning to soften, 3-4 minutes. Add onions and peppers to the casserole dish along with the drained canned diced tomatoes.
6. Whisk 12 eggs with the Italian seasoning in a bowl. Pour the eggs over the meat and veggies and stir to combine. Top with pepperonis.
7. Bake for 25-30 minutes until cooked through and the eggs are firm/set. Top with ranch dressing and enjoy! Store in the fridge for up to 5 days.

Breakfast Fried Rice

Dairy-Free, Gluten-Free, Nut-Free

Prep Time: 5 Mins // Cook Time: 15 Mins

Yield: 4

Recipe Type: Breakfast

This paleo breakfast fried rice is the best of both worlds: breakfast & Chinese food! Low carb cauliflower fried rice is combined with bacon and eggs to make the ultimate breakfast the entire family will love.

Ingredients

- 2 tbsp sesame oil
- 1 16 oz package frozen cauliflower rice
- 8 pieces sugar free bacon
- 3 eggs beaten
- 1/2 medium onion diced
- 1/2 cup diced carrots
- 3 cloves garlic minced
- 1/2 tsp sea salt more to taste
- 1/4 cup coconut aminos
- 3 green onions diced for garnish

Instructions

1. Cook bacon using my easy baked method (or method of choice!). Meanwhile, heat a large non-stick skillet over medium high heat.
2. Add sesame oil. Once hot, add the onion, carrots, and garlic. Sauté for 3-4 minutes until onion and carrots begin to soften. Add in the frozen cauliflower rice. Cook for an additional 3-4 minutes.
3. Add in the sea salt and coconut aminos and stir to combine. Push the mixture over to one side of the pan to make some room for scrambling your eggs.
4. Pour the beaten eggs into the pan and stir until cooked through, then toss them with the rest of the fried rice.
5. When the bacon is done, drain it on a paper towel and break it into 1 inch pieces. Add to the cauliflower rice and stir to combine. Serve topped with green onions and enjoy!

Pizza Egg Sausage Cups

Dairy-Free, Gluten-Free, Nut-Free

Prep Time: 15 Mins // Cook Time: 20 Mins

Yield: 12 Cups

Serving Size: 2 Cups

Perfect for brunch or meal prep! These Keto Pizza Egg Sausage Cups are so easy and so good!

Ingredients

- 1-pound Butcher Box Ground Breakfast Sausage (for nightshade free) or Ground Italian Sausage
- 1/4 cup Marinara Sauce (I used the nightshade free recipe from Made Whole)
- 12 small eggs (or 12 yolks only if you have large eggs)
- 1/4 cup nutritional yeast flakes
- 1 teaspoon Italian Herb Blend
- 1/2 teaspoon fine salt, divided
- minced chives

Instructions

1. Preheat oven to 350F.
2. Divide the sausage into 12 small balls, one for each mold in the muffin tin. Press it down then use a small bottle, like a spice bottle to press it in and make a cup. Sprinkle with 1/4 teaspoon salt.
3. Bake for 5 minutes. Remove from the oven (drain fluid if needed). Spoon 1 teaspoon of marinara in each sausage cup, then put the egg yolks or in each cup or crack the small eggs into them (it is okay if it spills over). Sprinkle with remaining salt, nutritional yeast and the herb seasoning over the eggs.
4. Bake for 15-20 minutes until eggs are done. The outer eggs will cook through and the inner cups will stay jammy! Just make sure the whites no longer jiggle. It's perfect for a crowd that has varied egg preferences.

5. Use a spatula to unmold the egg cups once they have cooled off a bit. Garnish with chives, add more salt to taste and drizzles of marinara... and dig in!

Calories: 468.3, Fat: 40g, Carbohydrates: 3.3g, Fiber: 0.9

Ice Cream Pre workout

Dairy-Free, Gluten-Free, Sugar-Free, Wheat-Free, Starch-Free

Prep Time: 15 Mins // Cook Time: 15 Mins

Servings: 4

Ingredients

- 4 Cans Coconut Cream (Organic)
- 2 Tsp. Dairy Free Vanilla Extract
- 1 Tbl Cinnamon
- 1/2 Cup Coconut Shreds (Optional) - Don't blend that, just stir into Ice cream when blended.
- 2-4 Tbl Sweetener of choice (Stevia, Monk Fruit_ or any other of your choice.
- 4-5 Scoops of the Vanilla Perfect Keto Protein Powder - Why perfect Keto?
- You can make this into a Chocolate flavor by just adding 5 Tbl of cocoa powder with 1 Tsp. Mint Extract instead of Vanilla Extract

Instructions:

1. Place a large pan in your freezer.
2. In a blender add the full ingredients, blend till nice and smooth.
3. Transfer the Ice cream to the large pan or Loaf pan that was in your freezer, Pour and transfer back into the freezer.
4. You can enjoy this amazing Ice cream after 30 minutes! Please let it thaw for about 5-10 minutes before eating and wet your Ice cream scoop for a smooth round texture!
5. Enjoy!

Mozzarella Cheese

Dairy-Free, Gluten-Free, Sugar-Free, Soy-Free, Egg-Free

Prep Time: 15 Mins // Cook Time: 1 hr.

Servings: 6

Okay, so this one here is my Favorite! It smells, Tastes and the text is like Mozzarella!! This cheese Melts, Shreds, Slices - You can use this in anything you like!

Ingredients

- 1 Cup Cashews (Soaked 35 Minutes before use)
- 1 1/4 Cup Nondairy yogurt. I got the Almond yogurt. (Low carb, Gluten free, Soy free, Dairy Free, Egg Free,) You can use any Flavor you like! You can make your cheese (Coconut, berry, Chocolate flavor)!!!
- 1/4 Cup Non Dairy Milk (Unsweetened Almond or coconut milk)
- 2 Tbl Coconut Oil (Melted)
- 2 Tbl Lemon Juice Squeezed
- 2 Tbl Grounded Chia seeds
- 1/4 Tsp. Garlic powder
- 2 1/2 Tsp. Nutritional Yeast
- 1 1/2 Tsp. Pink Salt (More for taste if you prefer)
- 1/2 Cup Water
- 2 Tsp. Agar Powder

Instructions:

1. Add Cashews, Yogurt, C oconut Milk, Coconut oil, lemon juice, garlic powder, Nutritional yeast, and salt in a blender and blend till smooth
2. In a pot add the water and warm over Medium heat. When hot whisk in the Agar powder, Grounded Chia seeds and whisk well till thickens.
3. Pour in the blended mixture
4. Stir well till becomes nice and stretchy and thick
5. Let in cool for a second.

6. Get your Brin ready. In a big mason jar add water and salt (Taste water and it should taste like the ocean) Then with an Ice cream scooper you are going to dig the cheese dump into brin, make sure the water is cold.

7. After you are going to put in fridge to cool for about a couple of hours before use.

8. Enjoy!

Coconut Flat Bread

Dairy-Free, Gluten-Free, Sugar-Free, Soy-Free, Nut-Free, Vegan

Prep Time: 15 Mins // Cook Time: 25 Mins

Servings: 3

These are so Delicious with simple, easy Ingredients that I'm sure you all have in your kitchen! They are very flexible, super soft, Delicious and extremely HEALTHY! Your entire family would love these and kids will really enjoy this flat bread because it's made from coconuts HA! plus they are easy to chew and won't hurt your teeth.

Ingredients:

- 1/2 Cup Coconut Flour
- 1 Cup Warm - Boiled Spring Water
- 2 Tbl + 2 Tsp. Psyllium Husk
- 1/4 Cup Coconut Oil (Melted)
- Pinch of Pink Salt
- Add your Spice (Paprika, Oregano, Lime Zest, Onion, Garlic Powder) anything you like.

Instructions:

1. Add the dry ingredients in a bowl.
2. Boil your water - Add Boiled water and melted coconut oil to dry ingredients.
3. Mix well - be careful because it can be a hot mixture from water.
4. Let the dough set for at least 5 minutes, start shaping and creating.
5. You can bake this in Oven on 350F or you can shape and fry in pan (No oil needed if in pan just be sure to flip every minute).
6. Once golden you can remove or if you want it darker.
7. Once cooled, Store in a zip lock bag and refrigerate.

English muffin

Nut-Free, , Diary-Free

Serving Size: 1/8 of the crust

Prep Time: 10 minutes // Cook Time: 22 minutes

Yield: Makes 8 Servings

Ingredients

- 1 1/3 tbsp. coconut flour
- 1 tbsp. oil (melted coconut oil, avocado oil)
- 1/2 tsp. baking powder
- 1 large egg
- tiny pinch of salt

Instructions

1. Add all ingredients to a 4x4 microwave safe bowl, tap on the counter a few times to remove air bubbles, and microwave for 90 seconds.
2. You can also bake in a oven safe container for 10 minutes at 375F

For 1 serving using coconut flour: 235 calories / 20g fat / 5.7 carbs / 3g fiber / 8g protein

Notes

1. Tap the container on the counter a few times to remove any air bubbles before you cook it
2. You could really use any nut flour that you want if you are allergic to almonds or coconut. For alternative nut flours like pecan four, you would use 3 tbsp. You use half the amount for coconut flour because it's not really a nut and it is very absorbent!
3. I found that a 4x4 microwave safe container made the perfect size piece of low carb bread that could be cut in half and stuffed with all the things
4. You could also use a round container that is 4 inches in diameter for a keto mug bread
5. If you would rather bake this in the oven, you can use an oven safe container and bake at 375 for 10 minutes
6. Toasting this low carb bread makes it have a much better texture. You could also use a skillet to toast it in some butter. Yum!

Vegan Chickpea Chocolate Chip Cookies
Gluten-Free, Nut-Free, Egg Free, Vegan

Prep Time: 10 mins // Cook Time: 20 mins

Servings: 16

Calories: 207 Kcal

An easy vegan cookie that is loaded protein, fiber and minerals thanks to the addition of chickpeas.

Ingredients

- 1 1/2 cups cooked chickpeas , or 1 (15 oz.) can, drained and rinsed
- 1/2 cup Gluten-Free oat flour
- 3/4 cup coconut sugar
- 3 tablespoons melted coconut oil
- 1 tablespoon vanilla extract
- 1/2 teaspoon salt
- 1/2 teaspoon baking soda
- 1 teaspoon raw apple cider vinegar
- 3/4 cup dark chocolate chips

Instructions

1. Preheat the oven to 350 and line a baking sheet with parchment paper.
2. Process the chickpeas, coconut oil and vanilla in a large processor until relatively smooth.
3. Add in the coconut sugar, flour, salt, baking soda and vinegar and blend until a smooth batter is formed.
4. Add in the chocolate chips and pulse briefly until incorporated.
5. Drop the dough by heaping tablespoons onto a lined baking sheet and use wet fingers to gently flatten each mound (they won't spread a lot on their own.)
6. Bake until the tops begin to crack and the edges are dry to the touch, about 18 to 20 minutes. Cool completely before serving.

Cinnamon Maple Cookies

Grain-Free, Dairy-Free

Prep Time: 10 // Cook Time: 15 mins

Makes: 18

Ingredients

- 1 1/2 cup flour
- 1/2 cup sugar
- 1/2 tsp. baking soda
- 1/2 tsp. salt
- 8 Tbsp. oil
- 1 Tbsp. vanilla
- 1 Tbsp. maple syrup
- 1 "egg" replacer (I use Ener-G egg replacer, found in most health food stores)
- cinnamon and sugar for coating

Instructions

1. Mix dry ingredients in a bowl. Mix wet ingredients in measuring cup (make sure they're blended well). Stir wet ingredients into dry ingredients.
2. Using hands, form dough into a big ball. (If it sticks together well, then it's the right consistency. If not, then add a bit of water and mix it well.)
3. Form dough into cookie sized balls and roll into cinnamon sugar mixture. Place on ungreased cookie sheet. Flatten each ball a little bit. Bake at 375 degrees for about 7 minutes.

Vegan yellow cake recipe

Grain-Free, Dairy-Free, Nut-Free, Paleo Egg-Free, Vegan

Prep Time: 10 // Cook Time: 30 mins

Ingredients

- 1 and ¾ cups (220g) All-Purpose Flour [I use equal parts GF all-purpose flour and quinoa flour - the quinoa flour helps it not be mushy]
- 1 cup (200g) Sugar [Stevie?]
- 1 tsp. Baking Soda
- ½ tsp. Salt
- 1 cup (240ml) Soy Milk
- 2 tsp. (10ml) Vanilla Extract
- ⅓ cup (80ml) Olive Oil (or other vegetable oil)
- 1 Tbsp. (15ml) White Vinegar

Instructions

1. Preheat the oven to 350 degrees Fahrenheit (180 degrees celsius)
2. Sift the flour into a mixing bowl.
3. Add the sugar, baking soda and salt and mix together.
4. Add the soy milk, vanilla, olive oil and vinegar and whisk it in.
5. Grease two 7 inch round cake tins with coconut oil and divide the mixture evenly between them.
6. Bake for 30 minutes

Keto Starch Free Custard

Starch-Free
Prep Time: 15 Mins // Cook Time: 20 Mins

Servings: 4 People

Ingredients:

- 2 Cups Coconut Cream
- 3-4 Tbl Golden Flax Meal
- 1 Tsp. Vanilla
- 2 Tbl Monk fruit sweetener or 1 Tbl Stevia
- 3 Egg Yolk

Instructions:

1. In a pot Medium heat, mix Coconut cream, Vanilla, Sweetener.
2. In a separate bowl, mix Egg yolk, Flax meal.
3. Add half of the heated liquid to the bowl that has the yolk etc., keep stirring.
4. Transfer the mixture in the bowl to the Pot and keep stirring till thickens up.
5. Transfer to cups or glass bowls.
6. Let it cool before refrigerating.

Chocolate Cake

Soy-Free

Prep Time: 15 Mins // Cook Time: 60 Mins

Servings: 6 People

If you love chocolate cake, then you'll love this chocolate cake! It's nice and soft very moist - Not dry at all. This will MELT IN YOUR MOUTH!!!!!

Ingredients:

- 1/2 Cup Coconut Oil
- 1/4 Cup Monk Fruit/Stevia Sweetener (Add more if you like, depending on taste)
- 3 Eggs Room Temperature
- 1 Tsp. Vanilla Extract
- 1 1/2 Cup Almond Flour (As find as you can get it)
- 1/3 Cup Coconut Flour
- a Pinch of pink Himalayan Salt
- 2 Tsp. Baking Powder
- 1/4 Tsp. Xanthan gum
- 1/3 Cup Cocoa or Cacao Powder
- 1 Cup Vanilla Almond Milk or Unsweetened

Instructions:

1. Pre heat oven 350F
2. Grease pan with Butter
3. Blend all Ingredients in blender for a couple of minutes till nice and smooth
4. Bake for 50-60 minutes
5. Let it cool for 10-15 minutes before cutting!
6. Enjoy!

Fudgy Keto Brownies

Dairy-Free, Gluten-Free, Sugar-Free, Soy-Free, Nut-Free, Egg-Free

Prep Time: 15 Mins // Cook Time: 35 Mins

Servings: 6

These are awesome! I have done this a few times and will continue to make them as the entire family love them

Ingredients:

- 1/2 Cup Melted Coconut Oil
- 1/2 Cup Cocoa Powder
- 3/4 Cup Monk Fruit/Stevia Sweetener (Add more or less depending on sweet tooth)
- 2 Flax Eggs (1 Tbl Grounded Flax Seeds and 3 Tbl Spring Water becomes One Egg - You Need Two)
- 1/2 Tsp. Pink Salt
- 1 Tsp. Espresso or Whisky or Non Dairy Milk
- 1 Tsp. Vanilla
- 1/4 Cup Chocolate chips of Cacoa Nips
- 1/4 Cup Coconut Flour

Instructions:

1. Pre heat oven 350F, in a sauce pan, Combine the Coconut Oil, Cocoa Powder, Chocolate –
2. Medium heat, Whisking until mixture is smooth and No Lumps
3. Take off heat and stir in the sweetener
4. Add in the Flax eggs and Vanilla, mix well, add in the coconut flour, salt, espresso , mix well
5. Pour in pan and Bake for 15-20 Minutes, let cool completely then Serve. Enjoy!

Low Carb Blueberry Muffins

Dairy-Free, Gluten-Free, Nut-Free, Sugar-Free

Prep Time: 10 Mins // Cook Time: 30 Mins

Servings: 2

Yield: 12

Serving Size: 1 Muffin

Ingredients

- 1/2 cup coconut flour
- 6 tablespoons psyllium husk
- 1 teaspoon baking powder
- 1/2 teaspoon salt
- 1/2 cup unsweetened sunflower seed butter
- 1/4 cup softened coconut oil
- 4 large eggs, room temperature
- 3 tablespoons yacon syrup or 1/3 cup honest syrup
- 1/2 cup non-dairy milk of choice
- 1 teaspoon vanilla extract
- 2 tsp. lemon zest
- 1 cup blueberries

Instructions

1. Preheat oven to 350F. Line a muffin tin with cupcake liners.
2. In a large bowl whisk together the coconut flour, psyllium husk, baking powder and salt.
3. In a separate bowl beat together the sunflower seed butter, coconut oil, eggs, syrup, vanilla and milk until well combined and creamy.
4. Add the wet mix to the dry mix and beat until a dough forms.
5. Add in the blueberries and lemon zest and use a spatula to fold in.
6. Use a ¼ cup scoop per muffin. Bake in the center rack for 25- 30 minutes or until the muffins have risen, round and golden on top.

7. Remove from the oven and let cool. Store in an airtight container at room temperature for up to 5 days.

Recipe Notes:

You can also use Zero Syrup which is vegetable glycerin (a sugar alcohol) and monk fruit or Honest Syrup made of vegetable fiber and monk fruit. While the latter is free of sugar alcohols which is ideal for some, it is high very high in total carbs (fiber). Use 1/4 to 1/3 cup in this recipe instead of Yacon Syrup.

Calories: 176.2, Fat: 12.7g, Carbohydrates: 10.4g, Fiber: 6.5g, Protein: 5.2g

Keto Blueberry Pancakes

Dairy-Free, Nut-Free, Sweetener-Free, Paleo

Prep Time: 5 mins // Cook Time: 12 mins

Yield: 6

Ingredients

- 1/2 cup fresh blueberries
- 4 large eggs
- 1/4 cup + 1 (maybe 2) tablespoons coconut flour
- 1 teaspoon baking powder
- 1/4 teaspoon fine salt (or 1/2 teaspoon coarse salt)
- 1/2 teaspoon Ceylon cinnamon
- 1/2 cup full-fat canned coconut milk
- 2 tablespoons buttery coconut oil

Instructions

1. Combine all of the ingredients in a blender (except the coconut oil).
2. Blend until smooth.
3. Use a spatula to quickly transfer the batter to a bowl, it will go from fluid to thick in a few minutes.
4. Let the batter sit in the fridge while you heat a large skillet over medium heat. IF your batter hasn't thickened to almost a paste-like consistency, add the extra tbsp. of coconut flour.
5. When the skillet or griddle have come to temperature add 1 tablespoon of coconut oil to it.
6. Measure out 1/4 cup of batter for each pancake. Cook 3 minutes then flip and cook another 3 minutes. Add more coconut oil to the skillet for the next batch of pancakes.
7. Makes about 6! Top with extra buttery coconut oil and fresh berries!

CALORIES: 305, FAT: 24, CARBOHYDRATES: 11, FIBER: 6PROTEIN: 10

Christmas Coconut Cookies

Dairy-Free, Gluten-Free, Sugar-Free, Soy-Free, Nut-Free

Prep Time: 15 Mins // Cook Time: 35 Mins

I love those!! You can decorate as you desire - Filled with healthy and Nutritious Ingredients, Real easy to make and I'm sure you have the ingredients already in your kitchen cabinet!

Ingredients:

- 3 Cups Coconut Shreds
- 1 Cup Melted Coconut Oil
- 3 Drops Mint Extract (or any other Extracts as you wish)
- 1/4 Cup Lakanto , Zero Free Maple Syrup (Keto Approved)

Instructions:

1. Melt the coconut oil
2. Mix all the ingredients together with your hands
3. Refrigerate for 30 minutes before shaping
4. start shaping
5. Add any decorations you like to make them more interesting like: Edible Glister, melted chocolate or Caramel (Recipe for my homemade caramel is under "Notes"
6. Store in a sealed container and put in fridge

Keto Pizza "Pocket"

Dairy-Free, Gluten-Free, Sugar-Free, Yeast-Free

Prep Time: 15 Mins // Cook Time: 30 Mins

Servings: 6

These are really delicious and it only takes 15-20 minutes in the oven! You can use these as "Bread" Sandwich buns for kids! Pizza crusts and the list goes on!!Simple yet delicious and Healthy Ingredients with a wide range of benefits.

Ingredients:

- 1 Cup Almond Flour
- 4 Tbl Psyllium Husk
- 2 Tsp. Baking Powder
- 1/2 Tsp. Black Pepper
- 1/4 Tsp. Pink Salt
- 1 Tbl Dried Dill
- 2 Tbl Apple Cider Vinegar
- 3 Egg Whites
- 1 Cup Warm Water or Non Dairy Milk (Hemp , Almond , Coconut)

Instructions:

1. In a bowl whip the Egg Whites just a little till you see bubbles.
2. Mix all the Ingredients including the Egg whites together very well.
3. Let the mixture sit for at least 5-7 minutes to absorb and thicken a bit.
4. Place a Parchment paper on a pan to start creating your shape. How big or small you want those to be is completely up to you!
5. Bake on 350F till light golden.
6. Remove from oven - Add your toppings, put back in oven at 375F for 10 minutes (Please keep an eye on them)

Dairy and Egg Free PIZZA!

Dairy-Free, Egg-Free, Vegan

Prep Time: 15 Mins // Cook Time: 35 Mins

Servings: 6

We just love Pizza and the only reason I made this delicious pizza/Pizza Crust / Homemade Pizza sauce / Pizza Topping and Best of all...

Pizza crust Ingredients:

In a Separate bowl please add:

- 4 Tbl Grounded Golden Flax Meal and 12 Tbl of Spring water , Mix with spoon a little (This will turn into Jelly and is your Egg Replacement)
- 1/2 Cup Coconut Flour
- 4 Tbl Organic Psyllium husk Powder
- 2 -3 Tbl Spice of your choice
- 1 Tsp. Pink Salt
- 1 Tsp. Grounded black pepper
- 3 Cloves Mashed garlic
- 2 Tsp. Baking Powder
- 1 Cup of Boiling Spring water

Instructions:

1. Mix everything together with a mixer and put onto your nonstick pan (I used a Parchment paper) - Made it easier for me.
2. Flatten this dough with a spoon.
3. This dough will expand a little more.
4. Pre-heat oven to 375F (Bake for 20 minutes, remove from oven , spread some coconut oil or Olive oil , Flip Crust and bake for an additional 10 minutes.
5. Remove from oven and add your Sauce , Dairy free cheese , Toppings, Dairy free cheese again and pop in oven again on Boil for 7 minutes (more or less, please check) till cheese nicely melted!

Sauce:

Avocado sauce: Avocado, lemon juice, Garlic, onions, Parsley, Dill, Avocado oil or Olive oil. Or you can use vegan mayo sauce

Toppings:

You can use any toppings you like! I used Mushrooms, Onions, Garlic, Olives, Nondairy cheese.

Sugar Free Low Carb Chocolate Crazy Cake

Egg-Free, Dairy-Free, Nut-Free, Gluten-Free, Sugar-Free

Prep Time 10 minutes// Cook Time 30 minutes

Servings 9 servings

Calories 162 kcal

Ingredients

- 1 cup sesame flour
- 1/2 cup ground flaxseed
- 1/3 cup unsweetened cocoa powder
- 1 cup Swerve confectioners
- 1 teaspoon baking soda
- 1 teaspoon baking powder
- 1/2 teaspoon salt
- 1 teaspoon white vinegar
- 1 teaspoon vanilla extract
- 5 tablespoons avocado oil
- 1/2 teaspoon chocolate liquid stevia
- 1 cup water

Instructions

1. Preheat your oven to 350 degrees F.
2. Line an 8 by 8 baking pan with parchment paper.
3. Whisk together the first 7 dry ingredients.
4. Make 3 depressions in the dry mixture, 2 small and 1 large.
5. Pour the vinegar in a small depression, the vanilla extract and chocolate stevia in the other small depression and the oil in the large depression.
6. Pour the water over the top and stir until smooth.
7. Spread the batter into the baking pan.
8. Place in the middle rack of your oven and bake for 30 minutes or until a toothpick in the center comes clean.
9. Allow to cool for 10 minutes then remove by holding the ends of the parchment paper. Place onto a cutting board to frost then slice.

You could make these into 12 servings for smaller pieces you total carbs will be 6 grams instead of 9.

Calories 162 Calories from Fat 99, Total Fat 11g 17%, Saturated Fat 1g 5%, Sodium 252mg 11%, Potassium 44mg 1%, Total Carbohydrates 9g 3%, Dietary Fiber 4g 16%, Protein 6g 12%, Calcium 1.9%, Iron 0.2%

Ella's Pumpkin Bread/Muffins

Dairy-Free, Gluten-Free, Soy-Free

Prep Time 10 minutes// Cook Time 15 minutes

Makes: 6

Ingredients

- 1 1/2 cups White Sugar
- 1 3/4 cups Flour (I used Gluten Free King Arthur 1:1 flour)
- 1 tsp. Baking Soda
- 1/4 tsp. Salt
- 1/2 tsp. Cinnamon
- 1/4 tsp. Nutmeg
- 1/2 cup Oil (I used Canola)
- 2 Eggs
- 1/3 cup Water
- 1 cup 100% Pure Pumpkin (I used canned)

Nuts Optional - Mixed In or Just on Top

Instructions

1. Preheat oven to 350 degrees. Add all of the dry ingredients into a large bowl. Whisk together to ensure they are mixed up.
2. Add the liquids, mix with hand mixer until combined.
3. Pour into greased pans (I sprayed with Avocado Oil) mini loaf pans, large muffin pans, cupcake tins, etc. Bake until done. The toothpick should come out clean.

Grain-Free Coconut Flour Tortillas

Dairy-Free, Gluten-Free, Sugar-Free

Prep Time 20 minutes// Cook Time 30 minutes

Servings 9 servings

Ingredients:

- 1/2 cup coconut flour
- 1/2 teaspoon grain free baking powder
- 1/4 teaspoon sea salt
- 1 1/2 cup egg whites (or 16 egg whites)*
- 3/4 cup almond milk

You can buy the free-range organic egg whites in the carton if you'd like, or use your left over egg yolks for ice creams and custard pies!

Instructions:

1. Mix all of the ingredients in a non-reactive bowl.
2. Let sit for 10 minutes so the coconut flour can soak up some of the moisture, and then whisk again. The batter should be runnier than that of pancakes, about the same as a crepe batter.
3. Heat a non-stick skillet over medium high heat and spray with oil or melt enough butter to coat the bottom and sides of pan.
4. Pour 1/4 cup of the batter into the pan, swirling the pan while you pour to ensure the bottom is coated and the tortilla is thin.
5. Once the bottom looks set (about 1 minute), carefully release the sides of the tortilla with a rubber spatula and turn over.
6. Alternatively, you could use a frittata pan, or turn the tortilla into another hot and greased pan or greased griddle. This may help the tortilla to stay in one piece. If your first couple break, don't fret and don't throw them away.
7. Add a little more coconut flour and try again, but keep the broken ones to use as filling if you're making enchiladas.
8. Spray the pan again, and repeat above steps until all the batter is used. Layer the tortillas on a plate and set aside until you're read to fill them and bake.

Low Carb Black Forest Cake

Dairy-Free, Egg-Free, Gluten-Free, Sugar-Free

Prep Time: 15 Mins // Cook Time: 35 Mins

Servings: 6

Ingredients

Pre heat oven to 350F

Berry Filling:

- 1/2 Cup Frozen Berries or Fresh
- 2-3 Tbl Spring water
- 1 Tsp. Xantham gum (Optional)

*Blend all the Ingredients together and put in your fridge till you're ready to use.

Frosting #1:

- 1 Cup Coconut Cream
- 2 Tbl Monk Fruit Sweetener or Stevia (Add more or less depending on your taste)

*Whisk and place in your fridge till you're ready to use.

Frosting #2:

- 2 Ripe Avocados
- 3-4 Tbl Non Dairy Milk (Almond , Coconut)
- Pinch of Pink Salt (1/4 Tsp.)
- 1 Tsp. Vanilla Extract
- 4 Tbl Cocoa Powder
- 2-3 Tbl Monk Fruit Sweetener or Stevia
- 20 Drops liquid stevia (Vanilla cream)

Cake:

- 1/4 Cup Almond Flour
- 1/4 Cup Flax Meal (Golden)
- 1 Tbl Psyllium husk powder
- 1/4 Cup + 1 Tbl Coconut Flour
- 1/4 Cup Monk Fruit sweetener or Stevia
- 15 Drops liquid stevia
- 1 Tsp. Baking Soda
- 1 Tsp. Cinnamon
- 1/2 Tsp. Baking Powder

- 1/4 Tsp. Pink Salt
- 1 1/4 Cup Non Dairy milk (Almond , Coconut)
- 1 Tsp. Apple cider vinegar
- 1 Tsp. Vanilla Extract

Instructions:

1. In a bowl, add all your dry ingredients and mix well till incorporated.
2. In a separate bowl, add all the wet ingredients and mix well till incorporated.
3. Add the wet ingredients to the dry ingredients till incorporated, pour into a greased with coconut oil glass baking pan. (I did this step Two times) because I wanted an extension layer cake. Remember… When you do a second batch… it must be in a separate baking pan to bake (your creating layers).
4. Bake for about 35-40 minutes.
5. Once done - remove and let it cool completely before adding any frosting to the cake!

You can mix it up a little, as you can see. I gave you the filling which goes in the center and I have two different types of "Frostings", use any way you like!

Keto Cookie Dough and Baked Cookie!

Dairy-Free, Egg-Free, Gluten-Free, Sugar-Free,

Prep Time: 15 Mins // Cook Time: 15 Mins

Servings: 6

Is my baked cookies from the cookie dough! No need for "Gums" No need for baking powders or baking sodas!

Ingredients:

- 3/4 Cup Almond Flour
- 2 Tbl Non Dairy Milk of your choice.
- 3 Tbl Nut or Seed Butter of your choice.
- 2 Tbl Lakanto Maple Syrup
- 4 Tbl Cacoa Nibs or Chocolate chips.
- 1 Tbl Cinnamon

Instructions:

1. Mix everything together in a bowl.
2. (If you want to leave it as a "Dough" then after mixed well, Store in your refrigerator for 1 hour before rolling them into balls).
3. Pre heat over to 350F and bake for 10-15 minutes, once light golden in color just remove. Let the cookies cool completely before eating.
4. Enjoy!

MAIN DISHES AND DINNER

keto game night chicken wings recipe

Egg-Free, Dairy-Free, Nut-Free, Gluten-Free, Sugar-Free

Prep Time: 5 minutes || Cook Time: 25 minutes

Yield: 12 wings (4 servings)

These chicken wings are cooked in a delicious keto-friendly marinade until sticky.

Ingredients

- chicken wings (with skin on) (1080 g)
- salt
- 2.6 oz. (73g) of Keto ketchup
- 1 1/2 Tablespoons (23 ml) coconut aminos
- teaspoons (10 ml) of balsamic vinegar
- 2 teaspoons (10 ml) of olive oil
- 2 teaspoons (10 ml) of garlic paste
- 2 teaspoons (10 ml) of ginger paste
- 2 green onions (10 g), sliced to garnish

Instructions

1   Preheat the oven to 355°F (180°C).

2   Spread the chicken wings out on a large roasting tray and season with salt. Place the tray into the oven for 15 minutes.

3   While the wings are baking, whisk together the ketchup, tamari, balsamic vinegar, olive oil, garlic paste and ginger paste in a small bowl.

4   After 15 minutes, remove the tray from the oven and use a pastry brush to brush the marinade onto the chicken wings. Return the tray to the oven for 5 minutes.

5   After 5 minutes, remove the tray from the oven and increase the oven to max. Baste one last time, using up all the marinade and return the tray to the hot oven for 5 minutes.

6   Season with salt and freshly ground and garnish with sliced green onions.

Net Carbs: 5 g

Serving Size: 3 wings Calories: 383 Sugar: 3 g Fat: 26 g Carbohydrates: 7 g Fiber: 2 g Protein: 28 g

KETO Pad Thai

Egg-Free, Dairy-Free, Nut-Free, Gluten-Free, Sugar-Free

Prep Time: 25 mins

Servings: 5 servings

Ingredients

- Stir-Fry Sauce
- 3 Tablespoons fish sauce Red Boat brand (unsweetened)
- 1 Tablespoon tamarind paste unsweetened
- 1/2 teaspoon sea salt
- Stir-Fry Assembly
- 5-6 medium-large size zucchini, spiralized into noodles
- 1-pound ground pork or prawns, (any meat of choice works great in this dish but cooking times will vary slightly, especially with seafood)
- 1 cup green onions chopped
- 1/2 cup scallion greens for garnish
- 1/4 cup lard or avocado oil
- 2 cloves fresh garlic minced
- 1 teaspoon sea salt
- 1 lime, cut in wedges

Instructions

1. In a medium bowl, combine and stir together sauce ingredients: tamarind paste, fish sauce
2. Heat large skillet or wok over high heat. Add 2 Tablespoons fat. Add pork, prawns or preferred meat and 1 teaspoon sea salt. Cook, stirring frequently, until no longer pink, about 10-12 minutes for pork or 2-5 minutes for shrimp. If you're using pork, use the spatula to break into small pieces as it cooks.
3. Remove meat to a dish while you continue cooking; set aside.
4. Add remaining 2 Tablespoons fat to hot pan (still over high heat). Add garlic and onions, and sauté until fragrant, about 2 minutes.
5. Add zucchini noodles, and cook 10-15 minutes, stirring and turning them over consistently (use tongs or 2 forks), until they're hot and slightly wilted. (Cooking times will depend on how big your pan is.
6. With a large pan you can cook the noodles evenly and quickly. If your pan is smaller and cramped, it will take more time and work to cook your noodles evenly.)
7. Add sauce ingredients. Stir to coat. Add meat, bean sprouts. Toss to mix and heat for about 2 minutes.
8. Serve noodles, topped with bean sprouts and scallion greens. Place a lime wedge to one side of each dish.

Turmeric Broccoli Chicken Roll Ups

Dairy-Free, Nut-Free, Gluten-Free, Sugar-Free

Prep Time: 30 min // Cook Time: 1 hr.

Yields: 8

Ingredients

- 4 boneless, skinless chicken breast halves
- one head of broccoli sliced into eight long stalks
- one 400 mL (13 1/2 ounce) tin full fat coconut milk.
- 1 tablespoon minced fresh ginger
- 1 whole large clove garlic minced
- 6 crimini mushrooms sliced
- 1/2 large onion diced
- 1 teaspoon salt. I use Himalayan or Celtic sea salt: buy from amazon.com
- 1/2 teaspoon powdered turmeric
- 1 heaping tablespoon coconut oil.

Instructions

1. Preheat the oven to 350 degrees F.
2. Over medium heat sauté onions and mushrooms in coconut oil until the mushrooms are a golden brown and the onions are translucent.
3. Turn the heat down to low and add the garlic and ginger.
4. Saute but do not let the garlic brown.
5. Add the coconut milk, salt and turmeric and simmer to thicken slightly.
6. Steam broccoli until almost, but not quite, fork tender.
7. Meanwhile place a chicken breast in a zip lock bag or in between two sheets of cling wrap and pound to a thickness of about 1/4 inch.

Assembly:

1. Place a broccoli spear on the chicken so that the flower end lines up with one edge of the flattened chicken. Place a second spear so that the flower end lines up with the other edge (imagine putting shoes in a shoe box end to end).
2. Spoon 1-2 tablespoons of the coconut milk sauce over the broccoli.
3. Tuck one edge of the chicken over the length of the broccoli and roll up.
4. Pin with toothpicks if necessary.
5. Slice through the middle so that you have two even halves of rolled up chicken with a broccoli flower poking out of one end.
6. Place in a large baking dish with the cut edge down and spoon the remainder of the coconut milk sauce over the roll ups.
7. Bake at 350 degrees F for 30 minutes.

Notes

- A rolling pin works well to pound the chicken breasts.
- When I made this I combined 1/3 cup cassava flour and mixed it with 1/4 cup coconut flour and salt. I then pressed both sides of the flattened breasts into the flour mixture. I think that this is just another step and that it is not necessary.
- This freezes well. Once thawed reheat in the microwave for 30-60 seconds.

Fat: 11 G, Protein: 29 G

One Pot Lasagna Skillet

Dairy-Free, Nut-Free, Gluten-Free, Sugar-Free

Prep Time: 5 || Cook Time: 20

Yield: 4 servings

This one pot lasagna features everything you love about lasagna without the grains or dairy! It's the perfect one pot meal for a busy weeknight that the whole family will love.

Ingredients

- 2 large zucchinis
- 1 lb ground beef
- 1 tsp salt, divided
- 2 tbsp avocado oil
- 1 white onion, diced
- 3 cloves garlic, minced
- 1 cup mushrooms, chopped
- 1 tbsp fresh basil, chopped
- 1 tbsp fresh parsley, chopped (plus extra for garnish if desired)
- 2 tsp dried oregano
- 1 cup spinach

Instructions

1. Chop the ends off of the zucchinis, and use a mandolin slicer or a peeler to slice the zucchinis into long, thin strips. Pat them down with paper towels to remove excess water and set aside.
2. Use a large, deep skillet to brown the ground beef. Season with 1/2 tsp sea salt, and set aside and drain excess fat when cooked.
3. Add the oil to the pan and heat. Cook the onions and garlic in the same pan on medium heat until the onions are translucent. Add in the mushrooms, zucchini slices and sauté for 4-5 minutes or until soft.
4. Add back in the ground beef, as well as the marinara sauce, and the remainder of the seasonings. Cook for a few minutes to combine the flavors, and stir in the spinach at the very end. Stir until the spinach has wilted.
5. Top with extra seasoning to taste, and serve!

Chicken and Shrimp Stir Fry

Dairy-Free, Nut-Free, Gluten-Free, Sugar-Free

Prep Time 5 minutes||Cook Time 20 minutes

Servings: 6 people

Calories 322kcal

There's always time to whip up a quick stir fry! Here's a recipe with chicken, shrimp, and broccoli that's AIP paleo, keto, and low carb friendly.

Ingredients

1. 2 tablespoons lard or coconut oil
2. 1 small onion sliced thin
3. 4 cloves garlic minced
4. 3 tablespoons ginger minced
5. 1 pound broccoli cut into florets
6. 1 pound chicken skinned, boned, and cubed
7. 1/4 cup coconut aminos
8. 10 drops liquid stevia
9. 1 pound shrimp fresh or frozen, peeled with tails
10. 1/4 teaspoon sea salt

Instructions

1. In a large skillet or wok, melt the lard (or coconut oil) over medium-high. Add onions and cook until translucent. Stir in the garlic and ginger and stir fry until fragrant.
2. Dump in the broccoli and stir fry for about 10 minutes.
3. Add the coconut aminos and stevia. Then, stir in the chicken, shrimp, and salt. Cook until shrimp is heated throughout (or turns pink if using uncooked). Serve hot over cauliflower rice.

Amount Per Serving (0.17 recipe)

Calories 322 Calories from Fat 153

Fat 17g26%, Saturated Fat 4g25%, Cholesterol 247mg82%, Sodium 989mg43%, Potassium 481mg14%, Carbohydrates 9g3%, Fiber 2g8%, Sugar 1g1%, Protein 31g62%, Vitamin A 575IU12%, Vitamin C 73.4mg89%, Calcium 160mg16%, Iron 2.9mg16%

Bulgogi (Korean Marinated Bbq Ribeye)

Dairy-Free, Nut-Free, Gluten-Free, Sugar-Free

Prep Time: 4 Hours || Cook Time: 10 Mins

Serves: 4

Ingredients

- ~1-1.5 pounds of sliced ribeye (you can get it pre-sliced at many Asian groceries (e.g. H-Mart), or ask your butcher/meat counter to slice it for you - or do it yourself, slicing to ~ 1-1.5mm thickness (probably easier if the meat is a bit frozen)
- Marinade
- 1 bunch scallions (reserve some for garnish)
- 1 large onion (half for marinade, half for cooking)
- 1 tb fresh ginger
- 6 cloves garlic (half a head)
- 2 tb coconut aminos
- 1 tb fish sauce (optional)
- 1 tsp sea salt
- 1 tb apple cider vinegar

- 1 asian pear (can sub apple or regular pear)
- 1-2 tb coconut sugar (optional, can sub honey)
- 2 tb olive oil or avocado oil
- ¼-1/2 c water
- avocado oil for cooking

Instructions

1. Chop or food process marinade ingredients to form a paste (or just blend Asian pear and add the rest of the ingredients in chopped). A
2. Add in bulgogi meat and enough water so that all the meat is covered by marinade. Leave to marinate for at least 4 hours or overnight.
3. Remove meat from marinade and drain/pat off with paper towels. Heat up 2 tb of oil in cast iron or good sauté pan over high heat.
4. When oil is hot add meat and ½ an onion (sliced) (do this in multiple batches if you can't fit all the meat in the pan so it has room to brown).
5. Cook for a few minutes until meat has caramelized. Garnish with scallions and serve immediately.

Chimichicken: Chimichurri Marinated Chicken

Dairy-Free, Nut-Free, Gluten-Free, Sugar-Free

Prep Time: 10 mins || Cook time: 40 mins.

Yield: 6 thighs

The combination of parsley, garlic, and oregano imparts loads of tangy, herby flavor into the chicken meat!

Ingredients

- 1 bunch fresh flat-leaf parsley, large lower stems removed
- 1/2 bunch fresh cilantro, large lower stems removed (omit if desired)
- 3 tbsp fresh oregano leaves (or 1.5 tbsp dried)
- 8 to 10 medium cloves of garlic
- 2 tsp unrefined salt
- 1/4 cup extra-virgin olive oil (this one is my favorite)
- 1/4 cup red wine vinegar (or coconut vinegar)
- juice of 1 lime
- 6 bone in, skin on chicken thighs
- 2 medium sweet potatoes or potatoes, peeled and cubed to 1" (sub low carb veggies for keto, turnips/radishes/etc.)
- 1 small onion, coarsely diced
- 2 tbsp extra virgin olive oil to coat vegetables

Instructions

1. Prepare the marinade by placing all of the ingredients in a food processor (I have this one), high powered blender, or in a container for an immersion blender (I use this one) and puree until a smooth paste forms. It should be fairly thick.
2. Generously rub each thigh with about 1 tbsp of the marinade, making sure to apply it on both sides and underneath the skin. TAKE CARE not to contaminate the marinade with raw chicken juices if you would like to use the extra as a condiment after the chicken cooks.
3. Place the thighs in a large glass dish with a lid and allow to marinate in the refrigerator overnight or for a minimum of 2 hours. (A plastic bag works, of course, but I prefer not to create the plastic waste. This marinade is so thick it will stick to the meat just fine in a glass dish). Store any leftover marinade in the fridge in a covered container to serve with the chicken.

4. Peel and chop the sweet potatoes and onion - you can do this at the same time you marinate the chicken if you like, just store them in another glass container with a lid in the fridge.
5. After the chicken has marinated, preheat the oven to 425F. Arrange the chopped sweet potatoes and onion in a single layer on a sheet pan and toss with the 2 tbsp EVOO. Sprinkle with salt to taste. Place the thighs on top, spacing them out evenly.
6. Bake until the juices run clear and the meat is cooked through at the bone, about 40-45 minutes (can vary depending on the size of the thighs, your oven, and the pan you used. Always cook chicken to temp! I use this thermometer)
7. Serve with the leftover marinade and enjoy! If desired, you can thin out the marinade with equal parts EVOO and vinegar to the desired consistency, or serve it as is.

Mongolian Beef

Dairy-Free, Nut-Free, Gluten-Free, Sugar-Free

This easy Keto and Mongolian Beef is so much healthier and tastier than takeout and it only takes 20 minutes to make

Prep Time: 5 mins || Cook Time: 15 minutes

Servings: 4 servings

Calories: 318kcal

Ingredients

- 1 lb flank steak sliced against the grain into thin, bite-sized pieces
- 1/2 tsp sea salt
- 2 tsp tapioca starch
- 1/4 cup avocado oil
- 4 garlic cloves minced
- 1 inch fresh ginger grated
- 1/3 cup coconut aminos
- 1/4 cup water
- 1 tsp fish sauce
- 1 bunch green onions cut into 2-inch pieces

Instructions

1. Season the beef with salt, then toss together.
2. Sprinkle with tapioca starch then toss until evenly covered.
3. Heat avocado oil in a skillet over medium high heat.
4. Working in batches, drop the beef in the oil a few at a time so the pieces aren't touching each other. Fry until dark and crispy, about 1 1/2 minutes on each side.
5. Remove from the skillet and set aside. Drain the oil from the skillet but leave about 1 tablespoon.
6. Add garlic, ginger, if using, into the same skillet.
7. Sauté until fragrant, about 1 minute.
8. Add coconut aminos, water, and fish sauce, and stir to combine.
9. Add the fried beef, and let it simmer for 3 minutes until the sauce is thickened.
10. Stir in green onions and simmer for 2 more minutes.
11. Remove from heat and stir in sesame oil.
12. Sprinkle with sesame seeds before serving with cauliflower rice.

Calories 318 Calories from Fat 180, Total Fat 20g 31%, Saturated Fat 4g 20%, Cholesterol 68mg 23%, Sodium 927mg 39%, Potassium 415mg 12%, Total Carbohydrates 6g 2%, Protein 24g 48%, Vitamin A 2.7%, Vitamin C 2.5%, Calcium 3.4%, Iron 10.5%

Basil Chicken Saute Recipe

Dairy-Free, Nut-Free, Gluten-Free, Sugar-Free

Prep Time: 10 minutes || Cook Time: 15 minutes

Yield: 2 servings

Ingredients

- 1 chicken breast (0.5 lb or 225 g), minced or chopped very small
- 2 cloves of garlic, minced or finely diced
- 1 cup (1 large bunch) basil leaves, finely chopped
- 2 Tablespoons (30 ml) water
- 1 Tablespoon (15 ml) gluten-free tamari sauce (or use coconut aminos)
- 1 Tablespoon (15 ml) avocado oil or coconut oil to cook in
- Salt to taste

Instructions

1. Add 1 Tablespoon of avocado or coconut oil into a large saucepan and add in the minced garlic. When the garlic has started to yellow, add in the optional diced chili.
2. Then add in the minced chicken.
3. Add in the water and cook until the chicken is cooked.
4. Add to the saucepan the tamari sauce and salt to taste.
5. Lastly, add in the basil leaves and mix it in. Serve with some Cauliflower White "Rice" for a delicious Asian dish that's Paleo, Keto, and AIP.

All nutritional data are estimated and based on per serving amounts.

Serving Size: 1 Large Plate Sugar: 1 g Fat: 10 g Carbohydrates: 3 g Fiber: 1 g Protein: 30 g

Zucchini Noodles with Avocado Sauce

Dairy-Free, Gluten-Free, Sugar-Free, Vegan

Prep: 10 mins

Servings 2

These delicious zucchini noodles (or zoodles) with avocado sauce are ready in 10 minutes. Besides, this recipe requires just 7 ingredients to make.

Ingredients

- 1 zucchini
- 1 1/4 cup basil (30 g)
- 1/3 cup water (85 ml)
- 4 tbsp pine nuts
- 2 tbsp lemon juice
- 1 avocado
- 12 sliced cherry tomatoes

Instructions

1. Make the zucchini noodles using a peeler or the Spiralizer.
2. Blend the rest of the ingredients (except the cherry tomatoes) in a blender until smooth.
3. Combine noodles, avocado sauce and cherry tomatoes in a mixing bowl.
4. These zucchini noodles with avocado sauce are better fresh, but you can store them in the fridge for 1 to 2 days.

Notes

Feel free to use any veggies or fresh herbs you have on hand. You can also spiralize other veggies like carrots, beet, butternut squash, cabbage, etc.

Any nuts can be used instead of the pine nuts, or even seeds.

Nutrition

Serving Size: 1/2 of the recipe Calories: 313, Sugar: 6.5 g, Sodium: 22mg, Fat: 26.8 g, Saturated Fat: 3.1 g, Carbohydrates: 18.7g, Fiber: 9.7g, Protein: 6.8g

Vegan Thai Soup

Dairy-Free, Gluten-Free, Sugar-Free, Nut-Free, Vegan

Prep: 10 mins || Cook: 15 mins

Main dish

Servings 3-4

You only need one pot to make this delicious vegan Thai soup. It's made with easy to get ingredients and you can add your favorite veggies.

Ingredients

- 1/2 julienned red onion
- 1/2 julienned red bell pepper
- 3 sliced mushrooms
- 2 cloves of garlic, finely chopped
- 1/2-inch piece of ginger root (about 1 cm), peeled and finely chopped
- 1/2 Thai chili, finely chopped*
- 2 cups vegetable broth or water (500 ml)
- 1 14-ounce can coconut milk (400 ml)
- 1 tbsp coconut, cane or brown sugar
- 10 oz firm tofu, cubed (275 g)
- 1 tbsp tamari or soy sauce
- The juice of half a lime
- A handful of fresh cilantro, chopped

Instructions

1. Place all the veggies (onion, red bell pepper, mushrooms, garlic, ginger and Thai chili), broth, coconut milk and sugar in a large pot.
2. Bring it to a boil and then cook over medium heat for about 5 minutes.
3. Add the tofu and cook for 5 minutes more.
4. Remove from the heat, add the tamari, lime juice and fresh cilantro. Stir and serve.
5. Keep the soup in a sealed container in the fridge for up to 5 days. You can also freeze it.

Notes

Feel free to use any type of chili you want.

Serving Size: 1/4 of the recipe, Calories: 339, Sugar: 5.3g, Sodium: 297.4 mg, Fat: 27.6g, Saturated Fat: 19.7g, Carbohydrates: 15.6g,Fiber: 3.2 gProtein: 14.8 g

Green Curry Kale & Crispy Coconut Tempeh

Dairy-Free, Gluten-Free, Sugar-Free, Nut-Free, Vegan

Serves: 4-6

NOTES: For the dressing component, I got real physical and just bashed everything up in a mortar and pestle. This may be sufficient for some, but depending on the intensity/freshness of your ginger and lemongrass, you may want to blend all of the dressing components instead, or do the whole thing up in a mini food processor and do yourself a little strain afterwards. Taste as you go and judge from there.

Ingredients

- 1 bunch of kale, leaves torn into bite-sized pieces
- 3 green onions, sliced + divided
- 3 big handfuls of cilantro leaves, divided
- 2 limes
- olive oil
- salt + pepper
- 2 inch piece of lemongrass (the bulb-ish part at the bottom of the stalk)
- 1 inch piece of fresh ginger, peeled
- 1/2-1 thai green chili (depending on your tolerance)
- 1 tsp ground coriander
- 1/2-1 tsp tamari soy sauce
- 1/2 cup full fat coconut milk, stirred
- 1-2 tbsp coconut oil
- 1 standard package of tempeh, cut into small pieces
- sesame + hemp seeds

Instructions

1. In a large bowl, toss the kale leaves, green parts of the sliced green onions (you'll be reserving the white parts for the tempeh + dressing) and two handfuls of cilantro leaves.
2. Squeeze the juice of one lime over the salad, add a bit of olive oil, some salt, and pepper. Toss everything together to combine, massaging the oil/lime juice into the kale leaves in order to soften them. Set this portion of the salad aside.
3. Cut 3 little strips of zest off of the remaining lime and cut them up rough. Throw them into a mortar and pestle. Add in about half of the leftover green onion whites.
4. Slice the piece of lemongrass, ginger, and chili and add those too. Finally, add the coriander and a bit of salt. Start bashing the ingredients together

until you have a chunky paste. I like to squeeze a bit of lime into the mortar to help aid this process along.

5. Once you have a decent paste, scrape it into a measuring cup and stir in the coconut milk along with the tamari. Chop up the remaining cilantro and and stir it into the mix as well. Check the dressing for salt, pepper and acidity level at this point. Adjust to your liking and set aside.

6. Heat the coconut oil in a large saute pan over medium. Add the remaining green onions and sauté until fragrant, about 30 seconds. Add the pieces of tempeh + some salt and pepper. Toss/stir the pieces of tempeh around here and there until all sides are browned and lightly crisp, about 8 minutes. It should sizzle and pop. Add a squeeze of lime at the end and toss them to coat.

7. Spoon the coconut dressing over the salad and finish with the crispy coconut tempeh pieces. Garnish the salad with sesame/hemp seeds and serve.

Creamy Pulled Pork Soup

Dairy-Free, Nut-Free, Gluten-Free, Sugar-Free

Prep Time: 15 minutes || Cook Time: 30 minutes

Yield: 2 servings

Ingredients

- 2 tsp (10 ml) coconut or avocado oil
- 1 medium onion
- 8 cloves garlic
- 1 1/2 lbs (680 g) cauliflower
- 1 tsp (5 g) fine sea salt
- 7 cups (1680 ml) chicken or pork broth
- 2 tsp (2 g) dried oregano
- 2 1/2 cups (300 g) pulled pork

Instructions

SOFTEN:

1. Heat a saucepan or dutch oven over low-medium heat. Dice the onion, then smash and peel the whole garlic cloves.
2. Add the oil, diced onion and smashed garlic to the pan, stirring through the oil to coat.

3. Allow the onion and garlic to soften, stirring occasionally to avoid any burning or coloring. Meanwhile, chop the cauliflower into evenly sized florets and add to the pan along with the salt and broth.

4. Increase the heat to medium-high and bring the broth to a simmer. Cook until the cauliflower is fork tender, about 20 minutes.

BLEND:

1. Remove the pan from the heat (turn off the burner) and carefully transfer it to a trivet and use an immersion blender to blend everything together until you have a smooth, creamy soup base.

2. Add the oregano leaves and return the pan to the heat.

SIMMER:

1. Turn the heat to medium and bring the soup back up to a simmer. If the soup is thicker than you prefer, add a little extra broth until the soup is the texture that you like.

2. Add the pulled pork and cook until the pork is hot all the way through before serving.

Crispy Ginger Lime Chicken Wings

Dairy-Free, Nut-Free, Gluten-Free, Sugar-Free

Prep Time: 15 mins || Cook Time: 70

Yield: 30

Crispy Baked Wings, Tangy Sticky Sauce!

Ingredients

- 15 pastured chicken wings (cut into 30 pieces)
- ½ tablespoon baking powder
- 1 tablespoon fine salt
- 1 tablespoon granulated garlic
- 2 tablespoons avocado oil

FOR THE SAUCE

- 2 tablespoons avocado oil
- 3 tablespoons coconut aminos
- 2 tablespoons apple cider vinegar
- ¼ cup bone broth
- ¼ cup juice from the orange
- zest of orange
- zest of 2 limes
- 6 cloves garlic, zested
- 1 inch nub of ginger, zested
- 1 tablespoon nutritional yeast
- 1 teaspoon turmeric
- 1 teaspoon dried dill weed
- ½ teaspoon garlic powder
- ½ teaspoon ginger powder

Instructions

1. Pre-heat oven to 250F. Place a rack over a sheet pan and lightly oil it. Pat your chicken dry.
2. Cut your wings per the instructions above at both joints. Store the tips for later use like broth.
3. Put all of the drumettes and wingettes in a large bowl and toss with salt, garlic and baking powder. Drizzle in the oil and toss again.
4. Line all of the chicken pieces up on the rack, you might have to crowd them a little, but make sure none of the pieces are actually touching.
5. Bake at 250F for 35 minutes. Then crank the oven up to 425F degrees. Bake for another 45-50 minutes until crispy, golden and delicious.

6. While the wings bake, heat a small sauce pot over medium heat. Once it is hot add in the avocado oil, coconut aminos and apple cider vinegar.
7. Bring it to a simmer while you measure out the rest of the seasoning and zest the fruit.
8. Add the orange juice and broth to the mix and bring it to a simmer again until the liquid is reduced by half and lightly coats a spoon.
9. Mix in the zest, yeast and seasonings. Stir until the sauce is like a thick, kind of chunky glaze. Remove from the heat. Go relax, you have some idle time.
10. When the wings are done remove them from the oven and toss in a large bowl with the sauce! Serve hot and enjoy.

Recipe Notes:

Baking Powder, not baking soda, you will need baking powder, but do not let this deter you from this recipe. I learned early on to make my own baking powder and it's a no-brainer.

To create Baking Powder

- Mix EQUAL PARTS: baking soda, cream of tartar and arrowroot starch.
- The best way to do this is to sift them all together. I usually mix up about ½ cup of each and store for all my paleo, AIP and other baking needs.
- This baking powder works GREAT and it's totally allergen friendly!

Serving Size: 5, Calories: 450g, Fat: 38g, Carbohydrates: 5g, Fiber: 1g, Protein: 42g

White Chicken Chili

Dairy-Free, Gluten-Free, Sugar-Free

Prep Time: 5 minutes || Cook Time: 25 minutes

Total Time: 30 minutes

Servings: 4 servings

Calories: 526kcal

This hearty and comforting White Chicken Chili comes together in 30 minutes, and it's perfect for a delicious weeknight meal!

Ingredients

- 1 onion
- 2 celery stalks
- 4 garlic cloves
- 1 tbsp coconut oil
- 1.5 lbs boneless chicken thighs or breasts
- 1 tsp dried oregano
- 1 tsp onion powder
- 1 tsp garlic powder
- 1 tsp salt
- 4 cups bone broth
- 2 limes
- 1 14-oz can of full-fat coconut milk

Optional: cilantro, green onion, plantain chips, avocado for garnish

Instructions

1. Dice onion, chop celery, and mince garlic cloves.
2. Heat coconut oil over medium-high heat. Add onion, celery, and garlic and cook stirring for 5 minutes.
3. Push the veggies to the side then add the chicken.
4. Season with dried oregano, onion powder, garlic powder, and salt.
5. Cook for 5 minutes, until chicken is browned on all sides.
6. Add the bone broth to the pot and squeeze in juice from limes, and bring to boil.
7. Lower heat to medium-low, and simmer for 10 minutes.
8. Remove chicken and transfer to a bowl, then use 2 forks to shred it completely.
9. Add the chicken back to soup, then add coconut milk.
10. Increase heat to medium-high, then boil for 10 minutes until the soup is slightly reduced and thickened.

11. Garnish as desired.

Calories 526 Calories from Fat 306, Total Fat 34g 52%, Saturated Fat 25g 125%, Cholesterol 161mg 54%, Sodium 856mg 36%, Potassium 825mg 24%, Total Carbohydrates 14g 5%, Dietary Fiber 4g 16%, Sugars 5g, Protein 44g 88%, Vitamin A 2.9%, Vitamin C 19.5%, Calcium 6.6%, Iron 18.8%

Crispy Bratwurst with Glazed Brussel Sprouts

Dairy-Free, Nut-Free, Gluten-Free, Sugar-Free

Prep Time: 3 minutes || Cook Time: 12 minutes

Yield: 5

Serving Size: 1/5 Recipe

Fast and easy healthy recipe! The perfect whole foods keto meal, made in 15 minutes!

Ingredients

- 1/4 cup coconut oil, for frying
- 5 fully cooked, pork bratwurst
- 1 pound Brussel sprouts
- 1 large sweet onion
- 3 tablespoons avocado oil
- 1/2 teaspoon fine salt
- 1/2 teaspoon garlic powder
- 3 tablespoons coconut aminos
- 1 tablespoon vinegar
- 1 teaspoon fish sauce
- 2 tablespoons pastured gelatin

Instructions

1. Heat two large skillets over medium heat.
2. While they come to temperature slice your bratwurst into thin slices, small dice the onion and shred the Brussel sprouts (if not using pre-shredded).
3. Add coconut oil to one skillet and the avocado oil to another. Let the coconut oil heat for another minute or so. In the meantime, add the diced onion to the avocado oil skillet and sauté for 2 minutes then add in the Brussel sprouts.
4. Add the bratwurst to the coconut oil and fry, stirring occasionally for 8-10 minutes. Simultaneously sauté the onion and Brussel sprouts until they are browned and tender. Mix in the salt and garlic powder to the Brussel sprouts.
5. In the small bowl combine the coconut aminos, vinegar and fish sauce, then add 2 tablespoons of gelatin on top and let it bloom. (Blooming gelatin: let it rest until the liquid has become a solid gel mass).
6. Lower the heat on the Brussel sprouts and mix in the gelled sauce mass to the veggie mix. It will melt and create a thick glaze sauce. Remove from heat.
7. Turn off the heat on the bratwurst skillet. Use a slotted spoon to remove the crispy bratwurst from the coconut oil. Serve together right away. Great with some mustard on top!

Recipe Notes:

- Time Saving Tip: Buy a bag of shredded Brussel sprouts instead of slicing them yourself!

Calories: 522, Fat: 46g, Carbohydrates: 16g, Fiber: 3g, Protein: 15g

Healthy Chicken Finger Recipe

Dairy-Free, Nut-Free, Gluten-Free, Sugar-Free

Prep Time: 15 mins || Cook Time: 25 mins

Course: Main Course

Cuisine: American, Paleo

Servings: 4 Servings

Calories: 345 kcal

I created this gluten free and paleo chicken finger recipe so I could continue enjoying a healthier version of one of my favourite foods, and make something familiar for my family too. Plus, this recipe is AIP compliant, Whole30, keto, and kid-friendly to boot!

Ingredients

- ½ cup coconut flour
- 2 teaspoons poultry seasoning (or sub for compliant spices like sage, thyme, salt and marjoram)
- ½ teaspoon sea salt
- 1 lb boneless skinless pastured chicken breasts
- ¼ cup avocado oil or melted ghee
- Coconut or avocado oil in a spray bottle (for misting)

Instructions

1. Preheat oven to 400F.
2. In a shallow bowl or on a plate, combine the coconut flour, poultry seasoning, and sea salt.
3. Slice the chicken breast into strips, and coat generously with avocado oil.
4. Dip the oil-coated chicken strips into the coconut flour mixture to coat.
5. Place the finished strips onto a baking sheet one-at-a-time. When all the strips are coated, mist them with a thin coating of oil (this step makes them even crispier).
6. Bake for 12 minutes, flip them over and mist with oil, before returning to the oven for another 12 minutes.
7. Enjoy with your favourite dip like organic ketchup or homemade paleo mayo!

Calories 345 Calories from Fat 198, Fat 22g34%, Saturated Fat 7g44%, Cholesterol 72mg24%, Sodium 454mg20%, Potassium 419mg12%, Carbohydrates 9g3%, Fiber 5g21%, Sugar 1g1%. Protein 26g52%, Vitamin A 60IU1%, Vitamin C 1.3mg2%, Calcium 16mg2%, Iron 1.2mg7%

Pressure Cooker Garlic "Butter" Chicken Recipe

Dairy-Free, Nut-Free, Gluten-Free, Sugar-Free

Prep Time: 5 minutes || Cook Time: 40 minutes

Yield: 4 servings

Ingredients

- 4 chicken breasts, whole or chopped
- ¼ cup Coconut OIl
- 1 teaspoon salt (add more to taste)
- 10 cloves garlic, peeled and diced

Instructions

1. Add the chicken breasts to the pressure cooker pot.
2. Add the oil, salt, and diced garlic to the pressure cooker pot.
3. Set pressure cooker on high pressure for 35 minutes. Follow your pressure cooker's instructions for releasing the pressure.
4. Shred the chicken breast in the pot.

Net Carbs: 3 g

Calories: 404 Sugar: 0 g Fat: 21 g Carbohydrates: 3 g Fiber: 0 g Protein: 47 g

keto lemon Blueberry Chicken salad

Dairy-Free, Nut-Free, Gluten-Free, Sugar-Free

Prep Time: 10 minutes || Cook Time: 10 minutes

Yield: 1 serving

Category: Dinner

Ingredients

- 10 blueberries or other berries
- 1/4 medium onion, sliced
- Large bag of salad leaves (approx. 125 g)
- 2 Tablespoons (30 ml) olive oil
- 2 teaspoons (10 ml) fresh lemon juice
- 1 large chicken breast (1/2 lb), diced
- 2 Tablespoons (30 ml) coconut oil to cook in

Instructions

1. Sauté the diced chicken breast in 2 tablespoons of coconut oil. Add salt to taste.
2. Toss the cooked chicken with the blueberries, onion slices, salad leaves, olive oil, and lemon juice.

Serving Size: 1 large bowl Calories: 490 Sugar: 1 g Fat: 42 g Carbohydrates: 5 g Fiber: 3 g Protein: 27 g Net Carbs: 2 g

Italian Burgers Recipe

Dairy-Free, Nut-Free, Gluten-Free, Sugar-Free

Prep Time: 5 minutes || Cook Time: 10 minutes

Yield: 2 servings

Grass-fed beef burgers are not only Paleo, and Keto, but they're also just really tasty and easy to make.

So, whip these up no matter what diet you're on. You can also switch out the seasonings or add in some vegetables to change the flavors.

Ingredients

- 1 lb of grass-fed ground beef (450 g)
- 2 Tablespoons of Italian seasoning (6 g)
- 2 Tablespoons of garlic powder (20 g)
- 1 Tablespoon of onion powder (7 g)

Instructions

1. Mix all the ingredients together well and form burger patties from the mixture.
2. Grill or pan-fry in coconut oil until done to your liking.

Calories: 640 Sugar: 3 g Fat: 48 g Carbohydrates: 9 g Fiber: 1 g Protein: 39 g

Sheet Pan Taco Bowls

Dairy-Free, Nut-Free, Gluten-Free, Sugar-Free

Prep Time: 10 mins || Cook Time: 35 mins

Ingredients

FOR THE SHEET PAN

- 3 tablespoons avocado oil, divided
- 2 cups cauliflower rice, frozen
- 1 pound bonesless skinless chicken thighs
- ½ red onion, sliced
- 1 bunch radishes, quartered
- 2 teaspoons pink Himalayan salt

- 1 teaspoon ground ginger
- 1 teaspoon dried parsley
- 1 teaspoon ground turmeric

FOR THE SAUCE

- 1 bunch cilantro, stems trimmed
- juice of 2 lemons
- 1 tablespoon apple cider or coconut vinegar
- 2 tablespoons coconut manna or coconut butter
- ½ teaspoon fine Himalayan salt
- 1 tablespoon nutritional yeast
- 1 tablespoon coconut aminos
- ½ cup avocado oil

TO SERVE

- 1 heart of romaine, shredded
- 1 ripe avocado, sliced

Instructions

1. Pre-heat the oven to 400F.
2. Drizzle one tablespoon of avocado oil all over a sheet pan.
3. One on side spread out 2 cups of frozen cauliflower rice.
4. Next to it, line up the chicken thighs so they are lying flat, snug but not overlapping.
5. In the space that is left arrange the red onion and radishes. Sprinkle the salt over everything, getting about 1 teaspoon on the chicken thighs.
6. Next add the remaining seasoning only to the chicken.
7. Then drizzle the rest of the oil all over the chicken and rice.
8. Put the sheet pan in the oven and roast for 30 minutes. Then broil for 5 minutes.
9. In the meantime, prepare the rest of the bowls. Shred the lettuce, slice the avocado and make the sauce.
10. Combine the cilantro, nutritional yeast, lemon juice, coconut manna, salt and coconut aminos in the blender, and blend on low until almost smooth. Then slowly drizzle in the avocado oil until the sauce is fluid. Remove from the blender and store in the fridge until ready to serve!
11. To assemble your bowls make a bed of romaine in two bowls. Then spoon the rice on one side, the radishes and onions on another. Find a spot for your avocado. Slice 2 chicken thighs per bowl. Then drizzle sauce over everything.
12. There will be extra sauce. Store it in the fridge and use as salad dressing!

Roasted "Loaded" Cauliflower

Dairy-Free, Nut-Free, Gluten-Free, Sugar-Free

Prep Time: 35 mins || Total Time:35 mins

Servings: 5 servings

Ingredients

- 2 heads cauliflower chopped small
- 10-12 ounces bacon
- 1 bunch green onions chopped, whites and greens separated into two piles
- 1 cup melting cheese (optional), grated leave out or if you can't have dairy; best options **include fontina, Port Salut and jack**
- 1 teaspoon sea salt
- several sprigs fresh thyme

Instructions

1. Preheat oven to 400 degrees Fahrenheit.
2. Spread bacon out on a large baking sheet (preferably a half sheet) Bake until done, about 15-20 minutes.
3. Remove bacon to plate, and set aside. Keep pan with fat.
4. Spread out cauliflower on pan with bacon fat. Sprinkle with sea salt. Toss well with two spoons, so cauliflower is well-coated with fat. (*At this

point, if you wish to make a one-pan dinner with roasted chicken, see instructions below in Recipe notes.)

5. Roast cauliflower about 22 minutes, or until tinged with brown on its edges.
6. Remove pan from oven. Add green onions' whites and optional cheese. Reduce oven temp to 200 degrees.
7. Put back in oven for 5 minutes.
8. Remove from oven. Transfer to serving dish with any pan juices. Top with green onions' greens and fresh thyme. Serve.
9. For individual servings, plate individual portions, top with green onions and thyme, and top with optional fried eggs for main course dish. For egg-free and AIP option, top with simple roasted chicken and serve with side salad.

Recipe Notes

- If you wish to roast chicken to make a one-pan dinner, we'll use the same bacon pan after Step 4: so...toss cauli in bacon fat with sea salt as Step 4 directs. Then put this cauli aside in a large bowl.
- Spread chicken legs (bone in, skin on, about 1.5 lbs) out on baking sheet. Roll them over a bit in the fat. Sprinkle with sea sal. Reduce heat to 375, and bake 10 minutes.
- Remove pan; increase oven temp to 400. Spread cauli on baking sheet all around chicken pieces, using a spatula to scrape any extra fat from bowl onto chicken pieces, basting them.
- Resume recipe with Step 5, baking cauli for about 22 minutes...

Creamy Tarragon Chicken Salad

Dairy-Free, Nut-Free, Gluten-Free, Sugar-Free

Prep Time: 30 mins ||

Serves: 2 Servings

Serving size: 1 serving

Ingredients

- 3 cups white chicken meat, chopped
- ¼ cup avocado oil
- 2 tbsp sherry vinegar
- 2 medium pears (1 1/2 cup total)
- ¼ cup red onion, 1/4th inch dice
- 2 tbsp fresh tarragon, minced
- 1 tsp sea salt

Instructions

1. Place chopped chicken in a large mixing bowl.
2. Mince the tarragon and add to the bowl, along with the pomegranate seeds if using.
3. Peel and chop the pears, placing 1/2 cup into the mixing bowl.
4. Blend remaining 1 cup of chopped pear, avocado oil, sherry vinegar, and sea salt until thick and smooth.
5. Pour the dressing over the chicken and toss around in the bowl until evenly coated then serve over a bed of leafy greens.

Chicken Casserole with Broccoli and Olives

Dairy-Free, Nut-Free, Gluten-Free, Sugar-Free

Prep Time: 10 minutes || Cook Time: 75 minutes

Yield: 6 servings

Category: Dinner, Lunch

Ingredients

- 2 chicken breasts (400 g), diced
- 2 heads of broccoli (900 g), broken into small florets
- 1 medium onion (110 g), diced
- 20 white button mushrooms (200 g), diced
- 6 slices of bacon, diced and cooked
- 20 olives, sliced
- 1–2 cups of coconut cream (240 ml), to cover the dish
- 3 Tablespoons of coconut oil (45 ml), to cook chicken in
- Salt, to taste

Instructions

1. Preheat oven to 350 F (175 C).
2. Cook the chicken breast in the coconut oil in a frying pan. Season with salt.
3. Add everything to a large baking pan and bake uncovered for 1 hour.

NOTES

All nutritional data are estimated and based on per serving amounts.

Calories: 472 Sugar: 5 g Fat: 35 g Carbohydrates: 15 g Fiber: 6 g Protein: 24 g

Easy Vegetable Beef Soup

Dairy-Free, Nut-Free, Gluten-Free, Sugar-Free

Prep Time 10 minutes || Cook Time 8 hours

Servings 8 people

Calories 223kcal

Craving something hearty and warming? And doesn't take a lot of prep time? This easy beef soup with vegetables, based on a Filipino recipe helps.

Ingredients

- 2 pounds beef shank 4 slices, 1-inch-thick per slice, bone in
- 400 grams red radish cut in half
- 600 grams napa cabbage (aka wombok) cut in half
- 300 grams eggplant sliced
- 6 cups beef broth
- 1 small onion chopped
- 3/4 teaspoon garlic powder
- 1/2 teaspoon Himalayan pink salt

Instructions

1. Wash beef in cold running water. Pat dry with paper towel.
2. Season beef with garlic, salt. Let it sit for 30 minutes, either at room temperature or in the fridge.
3. Place half of onions at the bottom of the slow cooker. Add 2 slices of beef, top with onions, add the remaining beef and onions. Pour beef broth.

4. Cook on high for 7 to 8 hours until beef is tender and falling off the bones.
5. Add radishes 30 minutes to one hour plus the eggplants and napa cabbage 15 to 30 minutes before turning off the slow cooker. Length of cooking the vegetables will depend on how soft you want them to be.
6. Enjoy this hearty soup with Eggplant Ensalata on the side and opt for some cauliflower rice.

Notes

- Look for beef shank with marbling bone marrow which adds flavor to the soup.
- Cut beef into bite sized pieces to cook faster.

Calories 223 Calories from Fat 45, Fat 5g 8%, Saturated Fat 1g 6%, Cholesterol 49mg 16%, Sodium 1112mg 48%, Potassium 984mg 28%, Carbohydrates 11g 4%, Fiber 3g 13%, Sugar 6g 7%, Protein 31g 62%, Vitamin A 245IU 5%, Vitamin C 34.2mg 41%, Calcium 127mg 13%, Iron 3.8mg 21%

Caramelized Balsamic Leek Turkey Hearts

Dairy-Free, Nut-Free, Gluten-Free, Sugar-Free

Prep Time: 30 mins || Cook Time: 5 mins.

Serves: 2 servings

Serving size: 1 serving

Ingredients

- 8 oz. turkey hearts
- 1/4 cup olive oil
- 3/4 tsp sea salt
- 2 tbsp balsamic vinegar
- 3 cups leek greens – chopped
- Fresh basil for garnish.

Instructions

1. Prepare turkey hearts by cutting each heart into fourths.
2. Heat 2 tbsp olive oil in a large pan over medium heat, and once hot, add leeks and allow-ing them to cook until tender and fragrant.
3. Remove cooked leeks from the pan and set aside for later use, then add remaining 2tbsp olive oil to the pan, turning the heat to low.
4. Add prepared turkey hearts to the pan, sprinkle with remaining sea salt and cover, allow-ing them to cook for 2-3 minutes until no longer pink in the middle.

5. Add the cooked leeks back into the pan and deglaze the pan with the balsamic vinegar, quickly stirring to scrape up any crispy bits from the bottom of the pan, then take the pan off the heat and serve, topping with basil sprigs.

Recipe Notes

- The basil is optional, but highly recommended, as it adds an extra pop of flavor especially loved by the individuals I served this dish to
- If you don't have turkey hearts, chicken hearts work equally as great.

Chicken Casserole with Broccoli and Olives

Dairy-Free, Nut-Free, Gluten-Free, Sugar-Free

Prep Time: 10 minutes ||Cook Time: 75 minutes

Yield: 6 servings

Ingredients

- 2 chicken breasts (400 g), diced
- 2 heads of broccoli (900 g), broken into small florets
- 1 medium onion (110 g), diced
- 20 white button mushrooms (200 g), diced
- 6 slices of bacon, diced and cooked
- 1–2 cups of coconut cream (240 ml), to cover the dish
- 3 Tablespoons of coconut oil (45 ml), to cook chicken in
- Salt, to taste

Instructions

1. Preheat oven to 350 F (175 C).
2. Cook the chicken breast in the coconut oil in a frying pan. Season with salt.
3. Add everything to a large baking pan and bake uncovered for 1 hour.

Calories: 472 Sugar: 5 g Fat: 35 g Carbohydrates: 15 g Fiber: 6 g Protein: 24 g

Asian Stuffed Mushrooms Recipe

Dairy-Free, Nut-Free, Gluten-Free, Sugar-Free

Prep Time: 15 minutes ||Cook Time: 15 minutes

Yield: 4 servings

Ingredients

For the mushrooms and stuffing:

- 20 medium white button mushrooms, remove the stem
- 1/2 lb (225 g) ground chicken (or use 1 chicken breast food processed)
- 2 green onions, finely chopped
- 2 cloves of garlic, minced
- 1 Tablespoon ginger, minced
- 2 Tablespoons coconut aminos (30 ml)
- 1 teaspoon salt

For the dipping sauce:

- 4 cloves of garlic, minced
- 4 Tablespoons of coconut aminos (60 ml)
- 1/2 teaspoon (2.5 ml) apple cider vinegar

Instructions

1. In a mixing bowl, combine the ground chicken, green onions, ginger, garlic, coconut aminos, and salt. Mix well.
2. Clean the mushrooms (remove the stems carefully). Using your hands stuff the meat mixture into the mushrooms.
3. You can either bake or steam these. (I steamed them for 15-20 minutes until the meat is cooked).
4. To make the dipping sauce, mix together the garlic, coconut aminos, and vinegar in a small bowl.
5. Serve the steamed stuffed mushrooms with the dipping sauce.

Calories: 105 Sugar: 6 g Fat: 2 g Carbohydrates: 12 g Fiber: 4 g Protein: 13 g

keto Lemon Blueberry Chicken Salad

Dairy-Free, Nut-Free, Gluten-Free, Sugar-Free

Prep Time: 10 minutes ||Cook Time: 10 minutes

Yield: 1 serving

Ingredients

- 10 blueberries or other berries
- 1/4 medium onion, sliced
- Large bag of salad leaves (approx. 125 g)
- 2 Tablespoons (30 ml) olive oil
- 2 teaspoons (10 ml) fresh lemon juice
- 1 large chicken breast (1/2 lb), diced
- 2 Tablespoons (30 ml) coconut oil to cook in
- Salt

Instructions

1. Sauté the diced chicken breast in 2 tablespoons of coconut oil. Add salt to taste.
2. Toss the cooked chicken with the blueberries, onion slices, salad leaves, olive oil, and lemon juice.

Net Carbs: 2 g

Serving Size: 1 large bowl Calories: 490 Sugar: 1 g Fat: 42 g Carbohydrates: 5 g Fiber: 3 g Protein: 27 g

Granola

Dairy-Free, Nut-Free, Gluten-Free, Sugar-Free

Prep Time: 10 minutes ||Cook Time: 10 minutes

Yield: 4 serving

Ingredients

- 2 cups fancy grade coconut flakes
- 1 heaping Tablespoon coconut oil
- 1 heaping Tablespoon coconut manna
- zest of an orange
- 1/2 teaspoon cinnamon
- 1 pinch salt

Instructions

1. Heat coconut oil and coconut manna until pourable. Mix in cinnamon and remove from heat.
2. In a bowl, add coconut flakes and drizzle the coconut oil mixture over it. Toss lightly with a spoon.
3. Add pinch of salt and zest the orange over the mixture and gently stir again.
4. On a parchment lined half pan (cookie sheet), evenly distribute the coconut flake mixture.
5. Bake in 350-degree oven for about 12-15 minutes. Be sure to stir a few times as it will quickly brown and when you stir the coconut it will help to evenly brown the mixture.
6. Remove from oven and let cool.

3-Ingredient Crispy Keto Chicken Thighs Recipe

Dairy-Free, Nut-Free, Gluten-Free, Sugar-Free

Prep Time: 5 minutes || Cook Time: 40 minutes

Yield: 4 servings

Ingredients

- 12 chicken thighs (with the skin on)
- 4 Tablespoons of olive oil (60 ml) or avocado oil
- 2 Tablespoons salt (30 g)

Instructions

1. Preheat oven to 450F (230C).
2. Rub salt on each chicken thigh in the mixture and place on a greased baking tray. Make sure the thighs are not touching each other on the tray. Drizzle the olive oil or avocado oil over the chicken thighs.

3. Bake for 40 minutes until the skin is crispy.

Net Carbs: 0 g

Turkey Sausage, kale & Pumpkin Soup

Dairy-Free, Nut-Free, Gluten-Free, Sugar-Free

Yield: Serves 8

Ingredients

- 1 lb sweet Italian turkey sausage
- 1/2 cup chopped onion
- 3 cups chopped pumpkin or butternut squash
- 4 cups chopped kale
- 4 cups chicken broth
- 4 cups water

Instructions

1. Cook sausage in a medium sized saucepan. Add onions and sauté until translucent. Pour the broth and water into the saucepan and bring to a boil – reduce heat.
2. Add the kale and pumpkin and simmer until the pumpkin is soft, about 20 minutes.

Calories: 118, Fat: 6g, Carbohydrates: 5.5g net, Protein: 11g

Leek and Cauliflower Soup with Coconut Cream

Dairy-Free, Nut-Free, Gluten-Free, Sugar-Free

Prep Time: 10 mins || Cook Time: 1 hour

Yield: 4

Ingredients

- 1 large leek (approx. 10 oz.)
- 1/2 cauliflower (approx. 10 oz.)
- 1/2 cup coconut cream, warmed + 2 additional Tablespoons (30 ml) for drizzling
- 3 cups chicken or bone broth
- Salt to taste

Instructions

1. Cut the cauliflower and leek into small pieces.
2. Place the cauliflower and leek into a large pot with the chicken or bone broth (or use a pressure cooker).
3. Cover the pot and simmer for 1 hour or until tender.
4. Use an immersion blender to puree the vegetables to create a smooth soup. (If you don't have an immersion blender, you can take the vegetables out, let cool briefly, puree in a normal blender, and then put back into the pot.)
5. Add in the coconut cream and salt to taste and mix well.

Thai Tom Saap Pork Ribs Soup Recipe

Dairy-Free, Nut-Free, Gluten-Free, Sugar-Free

Prep Time: 5 minutes|| Cook Time: 2 hours

Ingredients

- 1 lb pork spare ribs (get small ones if possible cut into 2-inch chunks) (you can use other meats if you prefer)
- 2 small red shallots, chopped into large chunks (or use 1 large yellow onion)
- 3–4 small lemongrass stalks, chopped
- 10 thick slices of galangal (or use ginger)
- 8 cups water
- 10 kaffir lime leaves (or use cilantro), tear them up
- Juice from 1 lime
- 2 Tablespoons fish sauce
- Salt to taste

Optional: chilis, green onions for garnish

Instructions

1. Place the pork spare ribs into a large pot of water and boil for 10 minutes. Pour out the liquid with the froth.
2. Pour approx. 8 cups of new water into the pot with the ribs, and add in the shallots, lemongrass, galangal, and salt to the pot.
3. Simmer on low heat with the lid on (so you don't lose all the great soup) for 1 hour.
4. Check the ribs are tender, then add in the kaffir lime leaves, fish sauce, the juice from 1 lime, and salt to taste.

Paleo Jello

Dairy-Free, Nut-Free, Gluten-Free, Sugar-Free

Yield: 2 cups of jello

Category: Dessert

Ingredients

- 1 cup of strawberries
- 1 cup of blueberries
- 2 tablespoons of gelatin powder
- 1 cup of water

Instructions

1. Puree the strawberries and blueberries in a blender or Vitamix.
2. Pour the pureed fruit into cups, filling each cup half way.
3. Place 2 tablespoons of the gelatin powder into a large bowl and add in 1 cup of cold water. Stir well. Then place the bowl into the microwave and heat on high for 1 minute. Mix well using a fork.
4. Pour the gelatin water into the cups with the fruit puree (almost filling each cup to the brim) and mix well.
5. Leave in the fridge to set for 3-4 hours.
6. Serve with a few slices of strawberries as garnish.

Ginger, Lemon Blueberry Detox Smoothie

Dairy-Free, Nut-Free, Gluten-Free, Sugar-Free

Recipe type: Beverage

Serves: 4

A refreshing and delicious smoothie that will aid your body in detoxing after all the holiday indulgences! With a sweet, tart taste you can't go wrong in resetting your body with this drink.

Ingredients

- 1 C. Organic, Frozen Blueberries
- 1 C. Organic Filler Free Coconut Milk,
- 1 Whole Avocado, peeled and pitted
- 1 Drop Therapeutic, Pure Ginger Essential Oil, or ½ inch peeled ginger root

- 1 Drop Therapeutic, Pure Lemon Essential Oil, or ½ Organic Lemon, juiced
- 1 Tlbs. Real, Pure, Organic Maple Syrup (optional)
- 2 Scoops Vital Proteins Collagen Peptides
- 1 C. Ice
- 1 C. Water

Instructions

1. Place all ingredients in a high power blender until all is combined and smooth. I use a Vitamix and it works perfectly.
2. This will make 4 small servings or 2 large servings.

Healthful Pursuit's Crispy Chicken Wings

Paleo, Gluten-Free, Dairy-Free, Sugar-Free, Corn-free, Grain-Free, Nut-Free, Egg-Free

Makes: 1 lb. (455 grams)

Serves: 4

These wings have the flavor of the classic "sticky" sesame wing, but with none of the sugar. Meaning you can eat a bunch and not have to worry about the corresponding sugar high! I enjoyed the tahini dip alongside these wings, but it's totally optional. If you want to go really crazy, you could toast the sesame seeds before sprinkling over top. Your choice!

Ingredients

- Marinade
- 5 tablespoons Ellyndale® Organics Sesame Seed Oil, divided
- 2 tablespoons coconut aminos
- 1 teaspoon balsamic vinegar
- 1 small garlic clove, minced
- 1-inch (2.5 cm) fresh ginger root, minced
- ¼ teaspoon finely ground grey sea salt
- pinch ground cayenne pepper
- 1 lb. (455 grams) chicken wings
- Optional Tahini Dip
- ¼ cup water
- 2 tablespoons tahini/sesame paste
- Toppings
- ¼ cup diced green onions
- 1 teaspoon sesame seeds

Instructions

1. Place 3 tablespoons of the sesame oil, coconut aminos, vinegar, garlic, ginger, salt and cayenne pepper in a large container with a lid, and whisk to combine.
2. Add chicken wings and seal with the lid. Set on the counter for 3 hours, or in the fridge overnight.
3. Preheat oven to 400°F (205°C) and set out your large cast iron pan, or line a baking sheet with parchment paper.
4. Reserving the marinade, place the chicken wings meaty side up on the prepared sheet. Drizzle with 1 tablespoon of sesame oil and transfer to the preheated oven.

5. Cook the chicken wings for 30 to 35 minutes, or until tops are golden.
6. To prepare the tahini dip, 5 minutes before the wings are ready, transfer the reserved marinade to a small saucepan and add water, tahini, and the remaining 1 tablespoon of sesame oil.
7. Cook on medium-low heat, whisking continually for 5 minutes, or until it has simmered for a minimum of 3 minutes.
8. Remove from the oven and transfer to a clean plate. Sprinkle the chicken wings with green onions and sesame seeds, and serve alongside the tahini sauce.

Unstuffed Cabbage Roll Soup

Gluten-Free, Dairy-Free, Egg-Fre

Prep Time 15 minutes // Cook Time 40 minutes

Servings 8 servings

Calories 160 kcal

Simple comfort food: an easy recipe for unstuffed cabbage roll soup with beef, tomatoes, and other veggies.

Ingredients

- 28 ounce can diced tomatoes
- 1 pound 90% lean ground beef
- 1 pound chopped green cabbage (about 5 cups)
- 5 cups beef stock
- 1 cup rice cauliflower
- 1/2 cup diced onions
- 1/2 cup diced carrots
- 1 tablespoon olive oil
- 1 1/2 teaspoons salt
- 1 teaspoon dried oregano
- 1 teaspoon dried thyme
- 2 tablespoons fresh chopped parsley

Instructions

1. Heat a 6 quart pot or Dutch oven over medium to medium-high heat. Add olive oil and ground beef, cooking for a few minutes until browned, breaking it apart as it cooks.
2. Add onions and carrots. Cook for a few minutes to soften, stirring frequently.
3. Add tomatoes (including the liquid in the can), cabbage, beef stock, cauliflower, oregano, thyme, and salt. Stir everything together.
4. Increase heat to bring to a simmer. Cover with a lid and decrease heat to maintain a simmer. Simmer for about 30 minutes or until cabbage is tender.
5. Uncover and stir. Top with parsley and serve while hot.

This recipe yields 6 g net carbs per serving.

Calories 160, Total Fat 7g 11%, Saturated Fat 3g 14%, Trans Fat 0g. Cholesterol 38mg 13%, Sodium 1080mg 45%, Potassium 110mg 3%, Total Carb 8g 3%, Dietary Fiber 2g 7%, Sugars 5g. Protein 13g, Vitamin A 22% · Vitamin C 48% · Calcium 3% · Iron 12%

6-Ingredient Spaghetti Squash Pizza Casserole

Dairy-Free, Egg-Free, Gluten-Free

Prep Time 10 minutes // Cook Time 25 minutes

This dinner casserole is low-carb, hearty, and healthy!

Ingredients

- 1 medium spaghetti squash cooked and shredded
- 1 small onion chopped
- 1/2 cup sliced mushrooms
- 1/4 cup sliced black olives
- 1 cup marinara sauce
- 1 cup vegan shredded cheese
- Salt and pepper to taste

Instructions

1. Preheat oven to 375F. In a medium-large sauté pan, cook onion and mushroom until soft and translucent.
2. Turn off the heat and mix in black olives, spaghetti squash, salt, and pepper. Stir in marinara until well combined.
3. Transfer mixture to a prepared casserole dish, top with vegan shredded cheese and any additional toppings.
4. Bake for 25 minutes or until heated through and cheese has melted.
5. Remove from oven and let cool slightly. Serve and enjoy!

Low Carb Pizza Casserole
Gluten-Free

Prep Time 10 minutes // Cook Time 35 minutes

Servings: 8 slices

Calories: 263kcal

A delicious keto pizza casserole that will be enjoyed by all. The gluten free crust is made with a simple mix of eggs, cheese, and cream.

Ingredients

- 4 oz. cream cheese softened
- 4 large eggs
- 1/3 cup heavy cream
- 1/4 cup Parmesan cheese grated
- 1/2 teaspoon minced garlic
- 1/2 teaspoon dried oregano
- 1 cup Parmesan, Asiago or Romano cheese any combination can be used
- 2 cups mozzarella cheese shredded and divided
- 1/2 cup low carb pizza sauce
- Pizza toppings optional

Instructions

1. Preheat oven to 350°Grease 13x9 inch baking pan.
2. In food processor or with electric mixer, combine cream cheese and eggs until smooth. Add the cream, Parmesan, garlic and oregano. Blend until ingredients are well combined.
3. Sprinkle the Asiago (Parmesan or Romano cheese and 1 cup of the mozzarella cheese in the bottom of the greased baking pan. Pour egg mixture over the cheese.
4. Bake for 30 minutes then remove from oven.
5. Spread with the pizza sauce. Add pizza toppings over top if desired. Cover with remaining 1 cup mozzarella.
6. Using oven broiler on high, broil a few inches from the heat elements until top is brown and bubbly.
7. Let sit for a few minutes before cutting.

Calories 263 Calories from Fat 18g, Total Fat 20g 31%, Saturated Fat 11g 55%, Cholesterol 143mg 48%, Sodium 586mg 24%, Potassium 140mg 4%, Total Carbohydrates 3g 1%, Dietary Fiber 0g 0%, Sugars 1g, Protein 15g 30%, Vitamin A 16.7%, Vitamin C 1.3%, Calcium 36.3%, Iron 5%

Paleo Beef with Broccoli

Paleo, Gluten-Free, Nut-Free, Dairy-Free

Prep Time: 15 Mins // Cook Time: 10 Mins

Servings: 4 People

Ingredients

- 1 lb. beef (sirloin, skirt steak, boneless short ribs…etc.)
- 1 to 2 heads broccoli, break into florets
- 2 cloves garlic, minced
- 2 pieces thin sliced ginger, finely chopped
- Ghee or cooking fat of your choice

Beef marinade:

- 2 tbsp. coconut aminos
- 1/2 tsp. coarse sea salt
- 1 tbsp. sesame oil
- 1/4 tsp. black pepper
- 1 tsp. arrowroot/sweet potato powder
- 1/4 tsp. baking soda

Sauce combo:

- 2 tbsp. coconut aminos
- 1 tbsp. red boat fish sauce
- 2 tsp. sesame oil
- 1/4 tsp. black pepper

Instructions

1. Slice beef into about ¼ inch thin. Marinate thin sliced beef with ingredients under "beef marinade". Mix well. Place broccoli florets in a microwave safe container. Add 1-2 tbsp. water. Loosely covered with a lid or wet paper towel and microwave for 2 mins. Cook until broccoli is tender but still crunchy. Set aside.
2. Heat a wok over medium heat w/ 1 ½ tbsp. ghee. When hot, lower the heat to medium, add garlic and ginger. Season w/ a small pinch of salt & stir-fry until fragrant (about 10 secs).
3. Turn up the heat to medium-high, add marinated beef. Spread beef evenly over the bottom of the sauté pan and cook until the edge of the beef is slightly darkened and crispy. Do the same thing for flip slide - about ¾ way cooked through with slightly charred and crispy surface.

4. Add "Sauce Combo". Stir-fry about 1 min. Add broccoli. Stir-fry another 30 secs. Toss everything to combine.

Peanut Butter Mousse
Dairy-Free

Prep Time: 15 Mins // Cook Time: 2 hrs.

Ingredients

- 1/4 cup Peanut Butter
- 2 tbsp. Coconut Oil (soft)
- 1 can Full Fat Coconut Milk (refrigerated 24 hours)
- 2 tbsp. Stevia
- 1/2 tsp. Vanilla Extract

Instructions

1. First in a medium size bowl, combine peanut butter and coconut oil, blend with hand-mixer till completely incorporated.
2. Next, open up the can of coconut milk and take out the solid (it will be right on top!) leaving liquid behind!
3. Add coconut milk solid, Stevia, and vanilla to peanut butter and whip until mixed thoroughly!
4. Place mousse into serving size dishes and put in the fridge for at least two hours. Garnish with a strawberry, and/or Lilly's chocolate chips and bon appétit! Dairy free keto Mousse!

Baked Asparagus
Dairy-Free, Egg-Free

Prep Time: 15 Mins // Cook Time: 35 Mins

Servings: 6

These are delicious just the way they are. Very healthy and healing for your gut. Asparagus has allot of health benefits and one main it's high in Fiber, High in Vitamins, Nourishes the digestive track and more!

Ingredients:

- 1-2 Bunches Organic Asparagus
- 5-8 Cloves Garlic
- 1 Tsp. Pink Salt
- 1 Tsp. Black Pepper
- 1 Tsp. paprika
- 1 Tbl Oregano
- 1 Tsp. Onion Powder
- 1 Tsp. Lemon or Lime Zest
- 2 Tbl Avocado Oil or Olive Oil Pure.
- Lemon or Lime Juice - However much you like.

Instructions:

1. Cut off 1 inch of the bottom root of the Asparagus and give it a good wash.
2. Place the Asparagus in the oven Pan, spread out.
3. In a little "Ceramic Mash bowl" place the Garlic with the spices and give it a good "Mash".
4. Add the wet ingredients to the mashed garlic, give it a good stir.
5. Pour onto the Asparagus.
6. Drizzle some Lemon or Lime juice (Which ever you prefer).
7. Bake on 350F for about 20-30 minutes. Don't over Bake (Don't let it discolor) Let there be a crisp to the Asparagus.
8. Enjoy!

Veggie Keto Burgers

Dairy-Free, Egg-Free, Gluten-Free

Prep Time: 15 Mins // Cook Time: 35 Mins

Servings: 6

These are so delicious and super easy to do! I make a huge batch and I freeze them individually in zip lock bags. If you want one or two because they are that GOOD and TASTY you can either toast **them or bake in oven.**

Ingredients:

- Optional: Spaghetti Squash or Sweet potatoes 1 Cup - Optional
- 4 Tbl Psyllium Husk Powder
- 1 Cup Chopped Parsley
- 1 Cup Chopped Cilantro
- 1 Cup chopped Kale
- 2 Cups Green Pea
- 2 Large Yellow or White Onions
- 3 Cups Zucchini
- 1 Cup Sun Dried Tomatoes
- 1/2 Cup Mushrooms
- 1 Cup Peppers
- 10 Cloves Garlic
- 3 Whole Lemons
- 2 Tbl Pink Salt
- 1 Tbl Black pepper
- 2 Tbl Paprika
- 3 Tbl Oregano
- 1 Tbl Dried Dill
- 1 Tbl Mustard
- 1/2 Cup Grape seed Oil or Olive Oil

Instructions:

1. Stir Fry everything together.
2. Add more or less spice as you like.
3. Blend everything together except for the Green Pea.
4. Mix everything well.
5. Form into Shapes
6. Bake on 375F for 12-15 minutes
7. Let cool them pack and store in Freezer.
8. Enjoy!

Ranch Dressing

Dairy-Free, Egg-Free, Gluten-Free

Prep Time: 15 Mins // Cook Time: 35 Mins

Servings: 6

Ingredients:

- 2 Cups Hemp Seeds
- 5 Cloves Garlic
- 1 Whole Lemon or 2 Whole Limes
- 3-4 Tbl Spring water
- 1/2 Tsp. Pink Salt
- 2 Tbl Oregano
- Lemon Zest (Optional)
- 1 Tsp. Onion Powder
- 1/2 Tbl Black Pepper
- 1/2 Tbl Dry Mint
- 1 Tbl Tahini (Which is, Grounded Sesame Seeds- becomes a paste)

Instructions:

1. In a blender, blend all the ingredients till nice and smooth.
2. Please Enjoy!

Zucchini Avocado Garlic Pesto Pasta!

Dairy-Free, Egg-Free, Gluten-Free, Wheat-Free

Prep Time: 15 Mins // Cook Time: 35 Mins

Servings: 6

Ingredients:

- 3 Organic Zucchini
- 2 Yellow or Red onions
- 8 Cloves Garlic
- 3-4 Avocados
- Mushrooms (Optional) or any other veggie to make it more interesting.
- 1/4 Tsp. Spice (Paprika, Cayenne , Dried Basil, Dried Mint , Dried Dill , Onion and Garlic powder , Oregano).
- Use any Spice you like and add as much you like, depending on your taste.

Instructions:

1. Spiralize the Zucchinis, set aside.
2. Slice the onions, Garlic, Mushrooms. (Set aside half the onions and garlic for the Pesto sauce and add the rest to the heated pan with the mushrooms, add a little bit of Avocado oil.
3. Let that caramelize on Medium heat.
4. Once that's been caramelized into a nice light golden color, add the Zucchini Pasta and stir fry that for about 5 minutes (Not too long).
5. Remove from heat and set aside.

Pesto Sauce:

- In a Nutribullet or blender of choice, add the Garlic, Onions, Avocados, Spice with Olive oil (1/4 - 1/3 Cup and with One whole Lemon) - Blend till Nice and smooth.
- You can add chopped up Walnuts , Pine Nuts , Macadamia Nuts in with this dish to make it crunchy*
- Once blended, pour a little bit at a time and mix.

Shrimp Curry Coconut Lime Cream

Dairy-Free, Egg-Free, Gluten-Free

Prep Time: 15 Mins // Cook Time: 25 Mins

Servings: 6

Shrimps are so good, but that depends how it's made, I love mine with spicey flavor and saucy of course!

These are so easy to make and basically all you need to be prepared for are the spices. You can enjoy this meal with a side of Cauliflower fried rice, steamed veggies or whatever you prefer.

First, I'm going to post my Curry "Paste" Recipe.

Ingredients:

- 1 1/2 Tsp. Cumin Seeds
- 1 1/2 Tsp. Coriander Seeds
- 1 Tsp. Brown Mustard Seeds
- 2 Tbl Avocado Oil
- 4 Garlic Cloves , Minced
- Size of Thumb Ginger , Grated
- 1 Red Chilli , Chopped and deseeded
- 1 Tsp. Turmeric
- 1/2 Tsp. Chilli Powder
- 1/2 Tsp. Chilli Flakes
- 1/2 Tsp. Pink Himalayan Salt
- 1 Tsp. Sweetener of choice Stevia , Monk Fruit , Swere
- 1/4 Cup Clean Water
- 1-2 Full Lime Juice
- 1 1/2 Tsp. Masala Garam (This is how you make this)
    - 2 Tbl Coriander Seeds
    - 1 Tsp. Cumin Seeds
    - 1/2 Tsp. Cloves
    - 1/2 Tsp. Cardamom seeds or powder
    - 3 Dried Bay leaves or 1 Tbl Powder
    - 1/2 Tsp. Cayenne Powder
    - 1/2 Tbl Cinnamon Powder

Blend all ingredients in a blender till nice and incorporated and pour in Mason jar, Seal tight, use when needed).

Instructions:

1. In a frying pan, (please do not add oil in this step). Toast the Cumin, Coriander and mustard seeds over medium heat until it's fragrant and the seeds start to pop.
2. Transfer the seeds that's in frying pan to a blender and blend till texture in fine.
3. In the same pan, add the Avocado oil and sauté the onions till they are caramelized, then add the minced garlic, ginger and chili - cook for about 5 minutes.
4. Then add the Masala, Turmeric, chilli powder, chilli flakes, salt and sweetener - Stir in the pan for about 5-8 minutes.
5. Lastly, add the finely grounded spices, water and Lime juice, mix to combine - IT'S GOING TO SMELL SOO GOOD!
6. Transfer everything to a food processor and blend till nice and smoothe.
7. Pour in Mason jar and add a bit of Avocado oil to retain the freshness and flavor.
8. Store in your fridge - Use when needed!

Instruction for the dishes

1. 1-2 Bags of Wild Shrimps, Washed and seasoned with a bit of salt and pepper. (You can cook the shrimps alone or you can add to the sauce. Whatever you prefer.
2. Heat 1 Tbl of Avocado Oil in a pan.
3. Add 1 Big Scoop of the Curry Paste.
4. 2 -3 Tbl Tomato paste.
5. Handful Chopped Parsley.
6. Sweetener of your choice , bring to a light boil and then add the 2 cans coconut Milk/Cream , Simmer and uncover on Medium heat for about 10-15 minutes .
7. Add Shrimps to the Sauce and cook for about 5-7 minutes, until cooked through.
8. Add the lime juice and check for seasoning if you thinks you like to add more seasoning feel free.
9. Serve with a side of Cauliflower Fried Rice.

Homemade Kale Chips

Dairy-Free, Egg-Free, Gluten-Free, Sugar-Free, Wheat-Free, Soy-Free, Starch-Free, Vegan

Prep Time: 15 Mins // Cook Time: 35 Mins

Servings: 6

We Love Chips, don't we? But taking care of our health, we can't eat Potato chips, why? High in carbs, Hidden sugars, Indigestion, Bloating, Gas and the list goes on.....! Guess what!?

Why can't we make Veggie chips that's Low in Carbs, Zero hidden sugars, Flavorful with amazing benefits! These are so delicious that take NO time to make - your entire family will enjoy, plus you can flavor them with any spice you like!

Ingredients

- 2 Bunches Organic Curly Kale (They do shrink, so you might wanna get more than two bunches).
- There aren't any measurements for the spice, add as much as you like- taste to see if you need to add more.
- Pink Himalayan Salt
- Paprika
- Black Pepper
- Nutritional Yeast
- Olive oil or Coconut oil or Avocado oil

Instructions:

1. Pre heat oven to 350F
2. Wash kale, Cut stem, Cut into squares (Not too small), Let Dry.
3. Drizzle desired Oil, Massage and Bake for 10-20 minutes (Please check and mix every 7 minutes to crisp evenly and to avoid burn).
4. Get your Salt/spice/Seasoning ready in a small bowl.
5. Once done, add your spice right away, mix.
6. Wait till fully cooled and serve!
7. Enjoy!

Chicken breasts stuffed with Mushroom and Spinach and creamed with Coconut Sauce homemade!

Dairy-Free, Egg-Free, Gluten-Free, Sugar-Free, Wheat-Free, Soy-Free, Starch-Free

Prep Time: 15 Mins // Cook Time: 35 Mins

Servings: 6

Ingredients:

Preheat over to 350F

- Chicken breasts (Organic , Grass Fed , Hormone and Anti-biotic Free)
- 2 Tins Mushrooms (Organic)
- 2 Spinach (In the plastic containers times Two)
- Two Packs of Tarragon
- A Few Stems Rosemary
- 2-3 Cans of Coconut Cream
- 1 1/2 Tsp. Black Pepper
- 1-2 Tsp. Pink Himalayan Salt
- 1-2 Cups Chicken Broth (Organic)
- 4 Head Limes
- 5-8 Cloves Garlic
- 1-2 Head Red Onion

Instructions:

1. Make sure you wash your chicken at all times before you start to cook with.
2. Gently Slice the Chicken Breasts, Flatten them down like "Connected wings" you're going to use a heavy "kitchen Hammer" hammer down (Not too thin).
3. Season the Chicken with Salt and pepper and your desires spice.
4. Grease the chicken with Avocado oil.
5. Chop up the spinach and mushrooms (Finely or your desired size). - Add seasoning on them.
6. Stuff the chicken with the mushrooms and spinach.
7. Have your pan or Iron Skillet ready with the chopped onions and Garlic - Add a bit of Avocado oil to the pan to prevent sticking and of course taste.
8. Add the chicken with the herbs to the pan on Medium high heat - every two minutes you are going to turn the chicken , then sauce are going to add 1-2 Cups of the Chicken broth, as you do this you are going to put the temperature on Medium heat. Let that simmer for about 5 minutes.

9. Add your coconut cream with the herbs, Lime (Add more salt if needed) for a few minutes 5-7 minutes let that simmer, then you are going to transfer this to the pre heated oven for about 20-30 minutes! .
10. You can enjoy this delicious meal with a big side of Salad and a nice Pesto Dip!

Please Enjoy!

Flaxseed Morning Muffins

Dairy-Free, Gluten-Free, Wheat-Free, Soy-Free, Starch-Free, Nut-Free

Prep Time: 15 Mins // Cook Time: 35 Mins

Servings: 6

These are great to have any time of the day because it's filled with healthy ingredients, high in Nutrition, filled with healthy fats, low in carbs and it doesn't contain any flours. I personally like to heat it up just a little in the oven, cut in half and add (Softened) coconut oil all over! Really DELICIOUS!!!

Ingredients:

- 2 Cups grounded Brown Flax Seeds
- 3/4 Tsp. Liquid Stevia (Vanilla flavor) or original.
- 3 Tbl Grounded Cinnamon
- 1 1/2 Tsp. Grounded Ginger
- 1 Tbl Baking Powder
- 1/2 Tsp. Pink Salt
- 5 Eggs
- 1/2 Cup Warm water
- 1/3 Cup Coconut oil or Avocado oil
- 2 1/2 Tsp. Vanilla extract

Instructions:

1. Pre-heat oven to 350F and prepare your muffin Tin with the paper cups.
2. In a bowl, add the flax meal, Cinnamon, Ginger, Baking powder, Salt and whisk till well combined.
3. In another bowl, add the Eggs, Water, Oil, Vanilla, Stevia and blend till well combined.
4. Transfer the liquid to the dry ingredients and whisk till well combined and fluffy (This should be very fluffy).
5. Allow to sit for a couple minutes.
6. Scoop out the batter to small muffin cups.
7. Bake for about 12-15 Minutes, until toothpick comes out clean.
8. Once done, Transfer to a cooling rack, allow to cool on rack for about 30 minutes before eating!
9. Please Enjoy!

Smoked Salmon Cucumber Dill Salad!

Dairy-Free, Egg-Free, Gluten-Free, Sugar-Free, Wheat-Free, Soy-Free, Starch-Free

Prep Time: 15 Mins // Cook Time: 35 Mins

Servings: 6

Dinner Ideas that's Keto, Low Carb and Healthy... Delicious of course! Well this here you'd want to have more. You can taste the Zest from the lemons, the Caramelized mushrooms with the smokiness from the Salmon. Yummy!

Ingredients:

- A pack of Wild Smoked Salmon
- 4 English Cucumbers
- Fresh Dill
- Lemon or Lime Zest
- 2 Sliced Avocados
- 1/2 Cup Sliced very thin Green Cabbage
- 1 Cup Fine sliced Romaine lettuce
- 1 Cup Fine sliced Green Kale
- 1 Cup Fine slices Mushrooms
- A head of fresh Red Onion
- 5 Cloves of Fresh Garlic
- 1/2 Lemon
- 1/2 Tsp. Salt
- 1/2 Tsp. Garlic powder
- 1/2 Tsp. Onion Powder
- 1/2 Tsp. Paprika Powder
- 1 Tbl Oregano
- 1 Tbl Basil

Instructions:

1. In a Pan, Caramelize the Onions, Garlic, Mushrooms with Avocado oil (Don't add too much oil because we are trying to caramelize this and just add a pinch of Salt on Low to Medium heat - Once done just set aside to cool down.
2. Shave the cucumbers and set that aside.
3. Slice up the lettuce, Kale, Cabbage and Avocados and Set that aside.
4. Add you spices or whatever spices you personally prefer in a small bowl and mix well to combine the mixture.
5. Zest the Peel from the Lemon or Lime and set that aside. Get your olive oil ready.
6. Squeeze the 1/2 of one Lemon or Lime, and set that aside.

7. Slice up your smoked Salmon.
8. Once you have prepared everything, Start adding all to a big bowl. (Make sure you mix very carefully).
9. At the end add your olive oil - Add as much as you like, Please taste and see you like to add more, but little at a time. Add your fresh dill for Garnish and a strong delicious Aroma taste.

Now if you want a creamier Sauce for your Smoked Salmon Salad you can make this sauce which I also Love so Much!

- 1 1/2 Cups Coconut Cream
- Zest of half a Lemon
- Juice from half a lemon
- 1/2 Tsp. Pink Salt
- A pinch of Black Pepper

Coconut Cream Berry Macaroons

Dairy-Free, Gluten-Free, Starch-Free, Nut-Free

Prep Time: 10 Mins // Cook Time: 1 hr.

Servings: 3

Don't we all love Macaroons? These are so delightful, with high good fats and super tasty. HA! Let's get down to the recipe! No Bake Macaroons!!

Ingredients:

- 2 Cans of Coconut Cream
- 1 1/2 Cups Coconut Shreds
- 1/2 Cup Berries
- 1 Tsp. Vanilla Extract
- 1/2 Tsp. Stevia (Add more or Nothing at all depending on your preference)

Instructions:

1. Toast the coconut shreds, till nice and light golden (They will burn fast so please be aware) -Toasting the coconut shreds will give a Nutty taste to the Macaroons.
2. Put all the Ingredients into a blender, and blend - Leave out the shreds.
3. Once all blended, with a spatula stir in the coconut shreds.
4. Scoop and shape as desired, put on a Tray and Refrigerate till nice and Hard... for about an hour (Depending on the Temp of your fridge)

Cabbage Chips

Dairy-Free, Gluten-Free, Sugar-Free, Soy-Free, Starch-Free, Nut-Free

Prep Time: 15 Mins // Cook Time: 35 Mins

Servings: 6

Don't we all love chips!? But we can't have because there are "Hidden Sugars", High in Carbs and you'll just feel like crap after eating, Our Stomach starts to expand, we start feeling more hungry.

So, I have created this amazing Cabbage chips that can be done more than one way and I'm going to explain.

Ingredients for the Coating sauce:

- 1/2 Cup Avocado Oil
- 1/2 Cup Sunflower Seeds or Pumpkin Seeds
- 1 Big Organic White or Yellow Onion
- 1-3 Carrots
- 3 Tbl Tahini
- 3 Tbl Apple Cider Vinegar
- 5-7 Cloves of Garlic
- 2 Tbl Lemon Juice
- 5 Drops Stevia
- 1 1/2 Tsp. Paprika
- 1 Tsp. Turmeric
- 1 Tsp. Pink Salt
- 1 1/2 Tsp. Nutritional Yeast (For a Cheesy Flavor)

Instructions:

1. Blend all Ingredients together till it's nicely smooth.
2. Set aside, this will be used to massage your cabbage and add a coating.

Cabbage Chips Ingredients:

- One large Organic Green Cabbage

Instructions:

1. In a Pot, fill clean water, add a pinch of salt and heat up.
2. Cut cabbage into long squares or depending on the shape you would like! Please be sure to remove the thick stem.
3. Place the cabbage in the hot water and let the cut up cabbages get a little tender... NOT too tender but once the cabbages start changing in color please remove and place immediately in ice cold water.

4. Once that's done. You are going to flat out transfer individually to a baking sheet. Do not stack them up together, they have to be separated.
5. Let them dry for about 30 minutes.
6. Massage the Sauce to the Cabbages.
7. Pre heat oven to 200F and bake for about Two hours , might take longer just check every now and then (You must be patient when making these amazing Cabbage chips)

French Fries" Keto

Dairy-Free, Gluten-Free, Sugar-Free, Soy-Free, Nut-Free

Prep Time: 15 Mins // Cook Time: 35 Mins

Servings: 6

Ingredients:

- A bag of Parsley Root
- 1 1/2 Tsp. Pink Himalayan Salt
- 1 1/2 Tsp. Paprika
- 1 1/2 Tsp. Garlic Powder
- 1 Tsp. Onion Powder

Instructions:

1. Add cold water in a bowl and set aside.
2. Slice the Parsley Root as thin or thick as you like. (I like to slice mine pretty thin)
3. After you slice the parsley root, put in the bowl filled with water.
4. Leave it aside for an hour.
5. Strain and put on Parchment paper, add your seasoning, Drizzle with Avocado oil and Bake on 350F for about 30-40 minutes (Please check to see if done and crispy.
6. Please check every 10-15 minutes and turn fries so it can bake and crisp up throughout.
7. To Fry: make sure you fry the Parsley root till nice and golden in color with Avocado Oil, then add your seasoning.

You can also use these Root vegetables to make fries:

Please note: Oils that have high smoke points are suitable for cooking (Avocado Oil, Coconut Oil, Macadamia Oil, Lard etc. When looking for ingredients, try to get them in their more natural form (Organic, without any unnecessary additives).

Homemade Keto Cereal

Dairy-Free, Gluten-Free, Sugar-Free, Soy-Free, Starch-Free, Egg-Free

Prep Time: 15 Mins // Cook Time: 55 Mins

Servings: 2

We all love eating cereal, right!? Well I sure did!! Sometimes I want to have cereal as a snack or after a workout but unfortunately chaining my lifestyle it was really hard finding something without any garbage in the ingredients. Like Sugar, Starch, Corn, Rice, Syrup etc. It would always make me feel sluggish, bloated and just tired. BUT I have created this amazing cereal that's filled with high, good fats, oils, protein, and Natural sweetener, filled with amazing vitamins, minerals and probiotics!! It also contains Collagen.

Ingredients:

- 1 Cup Macadamia Nuts (You can use other Nuts if you like)
- 1 Cup Pecans
- 1/4 Cup Sunflower seeds
- 1/3 Cup Cacao Nibs
- 1 Cup unsweetened coconut Flakes
- 2 1/2 Tbl Chia Seeds
- 1/4 Cup Egg Whites
- 2 Tbl - Options- Ghee Butter Melted, Vegan Earth Balance Butter Melted, Coconut Oil Melted.
- 3 Tbl Almond Butter (You can use any Nut Butters you like)
- 2 Scoops Perfect Keto Collagen Protein/MCT Powder
- 3 Tbl Stevia Powder or you can use any sweetener you like: Monk Fruit.
- 1/2 Tsp. Pink Himalayn Salt
- 1/4 Cup Cacao Powder
- 1 Tbl Cinnamon
- 1/2 Tsp. Grounded Ginger

Instructions:

1. Pre heat oven to 325F

2. Add all of the ingredients to a food processor, Blend on high to your desired consistency - I personally blended mine for about 25 seconds at first then I scrapped down the sides and blended again for an additional 40 seconds.

3. So in total your blending for about a couple minutes but please do at your own desired consistency, It should form a "Dough till it all comes together".

4. Pour to a baking sheet and spread not too thick or thin about 1/4 inches thick or you can shape them any way you like!

5. If you are not going to shape them and just flatten it out on your baking sheet, you are going to bake for 20 minutes, flip it over and bake other side for an additional 20 minutes , once it cools down a bit you are going to break it apart (as big or small as you like)

6. If the center is still moist? Turn your oven off and place it back to your oven for an additional 5-7 minutes just to crisp up.

7. Add to your Mason jar and set aside!

8. Pour in a bowl with none dairy milk!

9. Take it with you to work or school and have it as a snack!

For Egg-Free recipe

If you dissolve 1 tbsp. of flax seed meal into 3 tbsp. of water and bring it to a low boil, you can create a fluffier substitution for either egg whites or whole eggs in baking recipes.

However, be aware that flax seed in large quantities acts as a laxative. If your recipe calls for large numbers of egg whites, be careful how much flax seed meal you use as a substitute. Since it whips up fluffier than agar powder, use half agar and half flax seed substitutions for recipes that call for a large quantity of egg whites.

Keto Broccoli Wraps

Dairy-Free, Gluten-Free, Sugar-Free, Soy-Free

Prep Time: 10 Mins // Cook Time: 15 Mins

Servings: 1

These wraps are THE BEST EVER! They are delicious full of flavor, it doesn't crack at all, you can easily bend them, you can freeze them, and you can use this to make your Keto Pizza crust! How awesome and Nutritious are these ... HA!

Ingredients:

- 2 Heads of Organic Broccoli
- 4 Eggs
- 1 1/2 Tsp. Pink Himalayan Salt
- 1 Tsp. Paprika
- 1 Tsp. Garlic Powder
- 1 Tsp. Onion Powder
- 2 Tbl Oregano
- 1 Tbl Dried Basil

(With the spices, add more or less depending on your preference - you can only add the salt if you don't want to add the rest of the spices. if you want to add other types of spices please feel free. Those spice I love and goes well with the wraps)

Instructions:

1. Pre heat oven to 385F
2. Wash the Broccoli, blend in Food processor.
3. Whisk Eggs till well liquid forms.
4. Add everything into a bowl.
5. Mix Well, use Parchment paper or a silicone mat and Shape the wraps to desired form.
6. Bake for 10-15 minutes.
7. Let it cool to use.

Roast Beef in Slow Cooker

Dairy-Free, Gluten-Free

Prep Time: 15 Mins // Cook Time: 8 hours

Servings: 2

This is SO DELICIOUS and honestly you don't even have to do a lot of work! You can just put every ingredient in your slow cooker and do your thing away from the kitchen- HA! Tender, Juicy, fall off, Melts in your mouth, Grass Fed, Organic, Non GMO -- ROAST BEEF!

Ingredients:

- 2 LB Roast Beef (Organic , Grass fed)
- 1 -2 Tsp. Pink Salt
- 2 Tbl Black Pepper
- 1 Tbl Smoked Paprika
- 1 1/2 Tsp. Garlic Powder
- 1 Tbl Thyme
- 5 Leafs of Basil
- 3 Leafs of Sage
- 1 1/2 Tsp. Onion Powder
- 4 Tbl Avocado Oil
- 2 Cups Beef Broth (Organic)
- 1 1/2 - 2 Cups Pinot Noir Red Wine (121 Calories, 3.4 Carbs per 5oz) - Add less if you think it's too much.
- 8 Garlic cloves (Chopped up)
- 2 Tsp. Cold Water
- (Regarding the salt and spices, add more or less depending on your taste bud)
- 5 Stem Chopped , Celery (Organic)
- 3 Chopped Onions (Organic)
- 4 Long Carrots (Organic)

Instructions:

1. Marinate your roast beef with the spices.
2. Heat your pan with a little bit of oil add your roast beef to your pan just for it to become nice and golden brown on all sides, say about 3 minutes per side.. (Make sure you add rosemary to the pan with the oil as you do this to give it a little bit more flavor).
3. Let your roast beef sit for a bit before adding to the slow cooker.
4. Chop up your veggies, add Salt and pepper to them, and give it a good mix.
5. Add your roast beef to the slow cooker.
6. Add your veggies to the slow cooker.
7. Add the Beef broth and your Wine with the Sage and Basil Leafs.
8. Cover on High heat, once it boils, turn temperature to Low heat and let it simmer for 6-8 hours!
9. After this is done.
10. Remove the roast beef, set a side and add the sauce with the veggies in a blender. Blend that to become a thick beef sauce for your beef!
11. Once the beef is cooled down a bit... use two forks to separate the roast beef which will be so tender and will fall apart! Add your sauce!
12. On the side... Eat this with amazing Green Salad!
13. Enjoy!

Doritos

Dairy-Free, Gluten-Free, Sugar-Free, Soy-Free, Nut-Free

Prep Time: 15 Mins // Cook Time: 15 Mins

But the Crap that's in them is just horrifying! Instead I have decided to make my own homemade, healthy version that actually tastes like Doritos!

Ingredients:

- 1 Cup Golden Flax Meal
- 2 Tbl Almond Meal
- 1/4 Tsp. Pink Himalayan Salt
- 2 Tbl Dried Oregano
- 1/2 Cup Spring filtered water

Instructions:

1. Mix all the ingredients in a pan on Medium heat
2. Stir till Sticky
3. Move to a double parchment paper , put dough in between and roll out thin
4. Cut and shape as you wish
5. Bake on 325F for 10-15 min, till Crunchy and golden around the edges.

Ingredients for the Seasoning:

- 1 Tbl Paprika or Cayenne pepper
- 1 Tbl Onion powder
- 1 Tbl garlic powder
- 1/2 Tbl Nutritional yeast
- Fresh Lime

Instructions:

1. Once the Doritos are done
2. Squirt Lime on chips, one side or both side and sprinkle the spice mix .
3. Enjoy with any side of Dip!

Spring Inspired Dinner

Dairy-Free, Gluten-Free, Paleo

Prep Time: 10 Mins // Cook Time: 25 Mins

Serves 4

Ingredients

- 2 tablespoon extra-virgin olive oil
- 4 cloves garlic, minced
- 1 spring onion bulb, minced
- 1/4 cup chanterelle mushrooms, minced
- 2 pounds 85% lean grass fed ground beef
- 2 teaspoon @redmondrealsalt
- 1 lemon
- 4 ripe has avocado
- 2 teaspoons sumac season
- green part of spring onion, thin sliced

Instructions

1. Heat a 12" cast iron skillet over medium heat. When it comes to temperature add in the olive oil and minced garlic and onion. Sauté for 2 minutes then add in the chanterelles and sauté another 2 minutes.
2. Crumble the beef into the skillet and break it up with a whisk until crumbly and browned. Sprinkle with salt. Cook here, stirring occasionally for 10 minutes.
3. Spoon the beef into 4 bowls. Top each bowl with one diced avocado. Garnish with the sliced onion tops and the ground sumac!
4. The onion slices look like jalapeño and the sumac like red pepper, almost! Giving this #nightshadefree girl all the feels

Zucchini Dip

Dairy-Free, Gluten-Free, Egg-Free

Prep Time: 15 Mins // Cook Time: 10 Mins

That's way better then Hummus!

Ingredients:

- 4 Boiled Zucchini
- 1-2 Tbl Tahini (saseme seed paste)
- One whole Lemon Juice from one Lemon
- 3 Cloves Garlic Mashed
- 1/4 Cup Lemon Juice
- Cumin Spice
- Salt
- Black Pepper
- Paprika
- Dried Basil
- Dried Mint (Add as much or as little spice as you like, make sure you taste before adding more).

Instructions

All you need to do is blend everything together in a blender till nice and smooth.

London broil with Toasted Coconut Brussels

Dairy-Free, Gluten-Free, Sugar-Free, Soy-Free, Nut-Free, AIP

Prep Time: 10 Mins // Cook Time: 42 Mins

Yield: 4

SERVING SIZE: 1/4 recipe

An easy yet elegant meal the entire family will love. This sheet pan meal uses London broil for an affordable steak dinner!

Ingredients

For the Marinade:

- 1 teaspoon fine salt
- 1/2 teaspoon ground black pepper (omit for AIP)
- 2 cloves garlic, minced
- 4 sprigs fresh thyme
- 2 tablespoons avocado oil

Meat:

- 1– 1 1/5 pound London broil

Brussels sprouts:

- 1 pound Brussels sprouts, halved
- 2 tablespoons avocado oil
- 1/2 teaspoon fine salt
- 1 teaspoon onion powder
- 4 slices bacon, chopped
- 2 tablespoons coconut butter

Instructions

1. In a casserole mix all of the marinade ingredients. Add the meat and flip it around in the marinade to get it all over. Cover and set in the fridge overnight, turning over once before cooking (the morning of).
2. When ready to cook, remove the meat from the fridge, let it rest at room temperature in its marinade for an hour.
3. In the meantime, preheat oven to 400F.
4. Add your Brussels sprouts to a sheet pan, toss with oil, salt, and onion powder.
5. Arrange bacon pieces all over it and then distribute the coconut butter in little clumps all over everything.
6. Roast on the middle rack for 30 minutes at 400.
7. Leaving the Brussels sprouts in the oven, set oven to broil at the 30-minute mark, making sure your second oven rack is right under the broiler.
8. Add your London broil (in the casserole dish where it marinated- or move it to a sheet pan) and place it under the broiler. Cook for 4-5 minutes. Then use tongs to flip it over and cook it other 4-5 minutes.
9. Remove everything from the oven. Move the meat over to a cutting board. Let it rest for 8-10 minutes before slicing against the grain.
10. Transfer the meat to the sheet pan with the Brussels sprouts and set that bad boy on the dinner table. Dinner is ready! Dig in.

Calories: 298, Fat: 25g, Carbohydrates: 9g, Fiber: 3g. Protein: 12g

Pizza Egg Sausage Cups

Prep Time: 15 Mins // Cook Time: 20 Mins

Yield: 12 Cups

Serving Size: 2 Cups

Perfect for brunch or meal prep! These Keto Pizza Egg Sausage Cups are so easy and so good!

Ingredients

- 1 pound Butcher Box Ground Breakfast Sausage (for nightshade free) or Ground Italian Sausage
- 1/4 cup Marinara Sauce
- 12 small eggs (or 12 yolks only if you have large eggs)
- 1/4 cup nutritional yeast flakes (or parmesan cheese for those who can eat dairy)
- 1 teaspoon Italian Herb Blend
- 1/2 teaspoon fine salt, divided
- minced chives

Instructions

6. Preheat oven to 350F.
7. Divide the sausage into 12 small balls, one for each mold in the muffin tin. Press it down then use a small bottle, like a spice bottle to press it in and make a cup. Sprinkle with 1/4 teaspoon salt.
8. Bake for 5 minutes. Remove from the oven (drain fluid if needed). Spoon 1 teaspoon of marinara in each sausage cup, then put the egg yolks or in each cup or crack the small eggs into them (it is okay if it spills over). Sprinkle with remaining salt, nutritional yeast and the herb seasoning over the eggs.
9. Bake for 15-20 minutes until eggs are done. The outer eggs will cook through and the inner cups will stay jammy! Just make sure the whites no longer jiggle. It's perfect for a crowd that has varied egg preferences.

10. Use a spatula to unmold the egg cups once they have cooled off a bit. Garnish with chives, add more salt to taste and drizzles of marinara... and dig in!

Recipe Notes:

Calories: 468.3, Fat: 40g, Carbohydrates: 3.3g, Fiber: 0.9

Low Carb Blueberry Muffins

Dairy-Free, Gluten-Free, Nut-Free, Sugar-Free

Prep Time: 10 Mins // Cook Time: 30 Mins

Yield: 12

Serving Size: 1 Muffin

Ingredients

- 1/2 cup coconut flour
- 6 tablespoons psyllium husk
- 1 teaspoon baking powder
- 1/2 teaspoon salt
- 1/2 cup unsweetened sunflower seed butter
- 1/4 cup softened coconut oil, ghee or tallow
- 4 large eggs, room temperature
- 3 tablespoons yacon syrup or 1/3 cup honest syrup
- 1/2 cup non-dairy milk of choice
- 1 teaspoon vanilla extract
- 2 tsp. lemon zest
- 1 cup blueberries

Instructions

1. Preheat oven to 350F. Line a muffin tin with cupcake liners.
2. In a large bowl whisk together the coconut flour, psyllium husk, baking powder and salt.
3. In a separate bowl beat together the sunflower seed butter, coconut oil, eggs, syrup, vanilla and milk until well combined and creamy.
4. Add the wet mix to the dry mix and beat until a dough forms.
5. Add in the blueberries and lemon zest and use a spatula to fold in.
6. Use a ¼ cup scoop per muffin. Bake in the center rack for 25- 30 minutes or until the muffins have risen, round and golden on top.
7. Coconut Flour Blueberry Muffins (paleo, keto, dairy free, nut free)

8. Remove from the oven and let cool. Store in an airtight container at room temperature for up to 5 days.

Recipe Notes:

You can also use Zero Syrup which is vegetable glycerin (a sugar alcohol) and monk fruit or Honest Syrup made of vegetable fiber and monk fruit. While the latter is free of sugar alcohols which is ideal for some, it is high very high in total carbs (fiber). Use 1/4 to 1/3 cup in this recipe instead of Yacon Syrup.

Calories: 176.2, Fat: 12.7g, Carbohydrates: 10.4g, Fiber: 6.5g, Protein: 5.2g

Keto Tagalong Cookies

Dairy-Free, Gluten-Free, Grain-Free, Sugar-Free, Egg-Free

Prep Time: 30 Mins // Cook Time: 12 Mins

Servings: 2

These Tagalong cookies are like your favorite Girl Scout cookies, made even better because now they're cookies instead of bars! Cookies are gluten free, egg free, grain free, Sugar-Free, low carb, and a THM S. You can enjoy this treat without any guilt!–

Ingredients

Shortbread Cookie Layer:

- 3/4 cups almond flour
- 3 tbsp. Trim Healthy Mama Gentle Sweet or my sweetener

Optional: to make sweeter cookies use 1 scoop Better Stevia using the included teeny tiny spoon this comes to 45 mg of pure stevia if you are converting from another brand

- 1 tsp. gelatin
- pinch of salt
- 3 tbsp. cold butter cut into small pieces
- 1/2 tsp. vanilla
- 1/2 tbsp. water
- Peanut Butter Layer:
- 1/4 cup peanut butter
- 2-3 tbsp. Trim Healthy Mama Gentle Sweet or my sweetener
- 1 tsp. gluccomannan
- 1 tsp. peanut flour or almond flour

Chocolate Layer:

- oz. bar of 85% dark chocolate or sugar free chocolate chopped

Instructions

Shortbread Cookies:

1. Preheat oven to 325 and line a large baking sheet with parchment paper.
2. Put the almond flour, sweetener, gelatin, and salt in a food processor and pulse to combine. Add the butter and vanilla and pulse until tiny crumbs. Add the water and pulse until a dough forms.
3. Put the dough between two sheets of waxed paper. Roll it out about ¼ inch thick. Using a circle cookie cutter or an upside down glass (or any random circle object from your kitchen like my ice cream holder) cut out circles.
4. Lift gently with a spatula and put on a cookie sheet lined with parchment paper. Reroll the dough and make circles until you use it all. You will get about 20 cookies.
5. Bake 12 to 14 minutes or until golden brown. Let cool completely.

Peanut Butter Layer:

1. Meanwhile you need to make the peanut butter layer. Put the peanut butter in a small bowl and sprinkle the gluccomannan on slowly whisking between each sprinkling. Add the sweetener and peanut or almond flour. Whisk well.
2. Drop scant teaspoons onto a cookie sheet lined with wax paper equally the same number as your cookies. Freeze until firm.

Assembly:

1. Melt chocolate in the microwave. Start with thirty seconds and then stir. Continue microwaving for thirty seconds increments and stirring after each until the chocolate is 75% melted. Then just stir until it is all melted.
2. Put one frozen peanut butter disc onto each cookie. Drizzle with melted chocolate covering as much as possible. Using a knife or offset spatula make sure the sides are covered.

3. At this point I lift onto a different piece of waxed or parchment paper to get cleaner edges (you can reuse the parchment you baked the cookies on). Refrigerate to set the chocolate. Enjoy your Tagalong cookies!

Nutrition Facts

Calories 84 Calories from Fat 72, Total Fat 8g12%, Saturated Fat 3g15%,,Cholesterol 4mg1%, Sodium 31mg1%, Potassium 65mg2%, Total Carbohydrates 3g1%, Dietary Fiber 1g4%

Quick Pickled Ramps

Dairy-Free, Gluten-Free

Prep Time: 15 Mins // Cook Time: 30 Mins

Servings: 10

Calories: 50kcal

Ingredients

- 25 Ramp Stems Cleaned
- 1.5 cup Apple Cider Vinegar
- 1.5 cup Rice Wine Vinegar
- 1 cup Water
- 2` tbsp. Korean Chili Flakes
- 2 tbsp. Real Salt
- 2 tbsp. Lakanto Monkfruit Sweetener
- 1 tbsp. Mustard Seeds
- 1 tbsp. Celery Seed
- 1 tbsp. Dried Minced Garlic
- 1 tsp. Ground Ginger

Instructions

1. Clean and remove roots from ramp stems then place in a clean sterile jar
2. Combine all ingredients in a pot and bring to a simmer stirring every few minutes. Let mixture cool to room temperature before pouring into the jar making sure the ramps are fully submerged.
3. Store in your fridge for up to 2 months

Nutrition

Calories: 50kcal | Carbohydrates: 4g | Protein: 1g | Sodium: 1426mg | Potassium: 80mg | Fiber: 1g | Sugar: 1g| Vitamin A: 22.2% | Vitamin C: 5.6% | Calcium: 4.6% | Iron: 8.5%

Almond Ramp Pesto

Dairy-Free, Gluten-Free, Grain-Free

Prep Time: 10 Mins // Cook Time: 45 Mins

Servings: 15

Calories: 137kcal

Ingredients

- 6 oz. Ramps
- 3/4 cup Olive Oil
- 1/2 cup Roasted almonds
- 1/4 cup Grated Parmesan Cheese
- 1 tsp. Crushed Chili Flakes
- 2 tsp. Red Wine Vinegar
- Salt & Pepper to taste

Instructions

1. Once Ramp leaves are washed and patted dry rough chop the leaves into ribbons before adding to a food processor along with all other ingredients
2. Pulse food processor a few times before then continue to process for 10-15 seconds until the pesto reaches the consistency you prefer.
3. Taste for seasoning, then using a spatula scrape down the sides and pulse a few more times to fully combine
4. Scoop the pesto into small sandwich ziplock bags and press out as much air as possible before sealing the bag completely.
5. Store fresh for up to 2 weeks or freeze up to one year.

Nutrition

Calories: 137kcal | Carbohydrates: 2g | Protein: 1g | Fat: 13g | Saturated Fat: 1g| Cholesterol: 1mg | Sodium: 27mg | Potassium: 36mg | Vitamin A: 4.9% | Vitamin C: 1.6% | Calcium: 3.8% | Iron: 2.8%

Keto Chocolate Hazelnut Spread Swirl Muffins

Dairy-Free, Gluten-Free, Sugar-Free

Prep Time: 10 Mins // Cook Time: 30 Mins

Servings: 6

Calories: 255kcal

Make 6 muffins at 5 net carbs each.

These delicious Sugar-Free and low carb nutella swirl muffins feature a moist almond flour muffin base made in the blender. They're perfect for any ketogenic diet.

Ingredients

DRY INGREDIENTS

- 1 1/2 cups Almond Flour (130 g)
- 1 tbsp. whey protein isolate (optional)
- 1 tsp. baking powder
- 1/4 tsp. salt

WET INGREDIENTS

- 1/2 cup heavy cream
- 2 large eggs
- 1 1/2 tsp. vanilla extract
- 1/3 cup Sukrin :1(Sugar-Free granulated sugar alternative)

SWIRL TOPPING

- 6 tsp. Sukrin Sugar-Free Chocolate Hazelnut Spread (homemade Nutella)

Instructions

PREPARATION:

1. Preheat oven to 350 degrees F and place rack to the middle position. Line 6 regular sized muffin wells with parchment liners.
2. Warm the Sukrin Chocolate Hazelnut Spread in the microwave for 20-30 seconds or until it is easy to drizzle from a teaspoon.

METHOD:

1. Put the wet ingredients into the blender.
2. Then put the dry ingredients into the blender. Turn the blender on low and blend. Remove the lid and help the process out with a spatula.
3. Turn up to medium low and blend for 20 seconds or until the batter is smooth and nicely aerated.
4. Divide the muffin batter between 6 muffin wells, filling 3/4 full. Drizzle 1 teaspoon of the Sukrin Chocolate Hazelnut Spread over each muffin and swirl/mix with a toothpick.

BAKE:

1. Bake for 25-35 minutes or until the tops of the muffins are firm and springy to the touch but still sound moist.
2. Let cool for 5 minutes in the muffin tin then remove to a cooling rack. Refrigerate in an airtight container for 7-10 days or keep on the counter for up to 5 days.

NOTES

The protein powder helps the muffins keep their shape and not collapse in the middle once the hazelnut spread is added. I did not use it in the muffins in the pictures and you can see a dip where they collapsed a bit. They are still delicious, but are better with the protein powder. I'll leave the choice up to you.

NUTRITION

Calories: 255kcal | Carbohydrates: 6g | Protein: 9g | Fat: 22g | Fiber: 1g

Instant Pot Beef and Broccoli Soup

Dairy-Free, Gluten-Free, Paleo, AIP Friendly

Prep Time: 10 Mins // Cook Time: 20 Mins

Servings: 2

Yield: 3 servings

Serving Size: 1/3 recipe

Your favorite take out fake out made into a healthy soup!

Ingredients

- 1 pound steak tips
- 1 teaspoon baking powder (homemade corn free)
- 1 tablespoon coconut aminos
- 1 tablespoon Red Boat Fish Sauce
- 2 tablespoons ghee or coconut oil for AIP
- 3 cloves garlic, minced
- 2 teaspoons ground ginger
- 1 teaspoon fine salt
- 2 cups broccoli florets (1–2 crowns cut)
- 1 1/2 cup bone broth
- 2 tablespoon cashew butter or coconut cream for AIP

Instructions

1. Heat pressure cooker on sauté mode. While it heats toss the beef with the baking powder, let it sit for 2 minutes then add in the coconut aminos and fish sauce and toss to combine.

2. When the pot comes to temperature add in the ghee. The place the chunks of beef in the ghee, reserving the marinade. Sear for 3 minutes each side. Add in the marinade. Add in the garlic, ginger, salt and broccoli and stir well.

3. Add in the bone broth and stir well to deglaze the pot. Cancel the sauté function. Seal the lid and set to pressure cook on high for 15 minutes, when it's done cooking release the pressure manually.

4. Open the lid and use a slotted spoon or tongs to remove the beef chunks from the soup, set aside. Add in the cashew cream and use an immersion blender to blend the broccoli mix until smooth.

5. Add the beef chunks back in and stir. Serve hot!cTop with a fried egg, sesame oil or sesame seeds, green onions or enjoy as is!

Nutrition

CALORIES: 345.9, FAT: 17.7g, CARBOHYDRATES: 8.1g, FIBER: 2.3g, PROTEIN: 40.6g

Pressure Cooker "Cheesy" Chicken & Zoodles

Dairy-Free, Gluten-Free, Paleo, AIP

Prep Time: 5 Mins // Cook Time: 35 Mins

Serves: 4!

Serving Size: 1/4 Recipe

Ingredients

- 1.5lb boneless, skinless thighs
- 1.5 tbsp. Tin Star brown butter ghee, use tallow for AIP
- 1.5–2 cups sliced leeks (or sweet onion)
- 2 tbsp. Apple cider vinegar
- 1/2 cup sliced carrots
- 4 garlic cloves (or 1 tsp. garlic powder)
- 1 tbsp. Great Lakes Beef gelatin
- 1/2 cup nutritional yeast
- 1/2 tsp. salt
- 1 tsp. Italian herb blend *rosemary, thyme, oregano, basil, sage
- 1 tsp. rosemary
- 2 large zucchini
- 1 clove garlic
- 1 bunch broccoli rabe
- a fist full of greens (arugula, baby kale, spinach)
- extra ghee (or other cooking fat) and salt for vegetables
- optional: 2 slices prosciutto or bacon

Instructions

1. Heat pressure cooker in sauté mode, add in the ghee (or tallow).
2. As it heats, slice and add leeks, carrots and garlic to the pressure cooker.
3. You don't have to give them a proper browning, but this way the leek caramelize a bit beforehand.

4. Once all the veggies are in, add in the vinegar, then the herbs, the chicken and lastly the yeast and beef gelatin.

5. Stir well.

6. Set to pressure cook, poultry mode.

7. My pressure cooker takes about 25 minutes.

8. In that time spiralize 2 zucchini, spread the zoodles out over kitchen towels and sprinkle with salt.

9. Cover with paper towel and pat down. Set aside.

10. Mince a few cloves garlic.

11. Dice up some broccoli or broccoli rabe and sauté in a skillet on high heat with more ghee (or tallow).

12. Stir often until the edges are browned, you can also add some prosciutto or bacon to the mix.

13. Turn heat down and add a fist full of greens (spinach, kale or arugula). Mix in.

14. When wilted, remove from heat. Sprinkle with salt.

15. When chicken is done & pot has released pressure, remove the insert from the pressure cooker and set it under a fan to cool off a bit, at this point you can also shred the chicken carefully with a fork.

16. You don't want it to get cold, but as the sauce cools it will thicken to a gravy like consistency (like melted cheese!).

17. Toss zoodles and broccoli mix in a large bowl.

18. Spoon chicken over vegetables generously.

19. Use tongs to plate it.

Nutrition

CALORIES: 381, FAT: 16g, CARBOHYDRATES: 17g, FIBER: 7g, PROTEIN: 45g

Creamy Ham Soup

Dairy-Free, Gluten-Free, Grain-Free

Prep Time: 10 Mins // Cook Time: 50 Mins

Servings: 2

Yield: 6 servings

Serving Size: 1/6 Recipe

Ingredients

- 1 large head cauliflower (4 cups florets)
- 3 cups bone broth
- 1 smoked ham hock or shank, bone in (about 1-2lbs)
- 2 bay leaves
- ¼ tsp. nutmeg (optional)
- 1 teaspoon onion powder (optional)

Instructions

1. Cut the cauliflower into 4-5 pieces. Place them in your slow cooker or pressure cooker. Add in the ham hock, bay leaves, nutmeg and broth. If the ham and/or cauliflower are protruding a lot from the broth, add in water until they are just submerged.

2. For Pressure Cooker: Set to HIGH FOR 50 MINUTES.

3. For Slow Cooker: Set to HIGH FOR 4 HOURS.

4. When it is done, the cauliflower should be tender and mostly falling apart.

5. Use tongs and/or a slotted spoon to fish out the ham hock. It will be falling apart too. Set it in a small bowl and shred it. Remove the bone and any large pieces of fat.

6. Transfer most of the liquid along with most of the cauliflower, aim for the bigger pieces, to your blender. Add in a few pieces of ham. Blend until almost smooth. It should be a beige color, with pearl sized cauliflower pieces and specks of pink.

7. Pour this mix back in to the slow cooker or pressure cooker, add in the shredded ham. Mix well. It should be creamy with chunks of cauliflower about the size of beans (you see!) and pieces of ham.

8. If you want the soup thicker or thinner you can add more broth or water, alternatively you can reduce it (bring it to a simmer until desired consistency is achieved).

9. Serve and salt to taste. As I mentioned above, the ham is pretty salty, asis the seedy seasoning. Add your toppings and salt as needed when you serve the soup.

10. Store in an airtight container in the fridge for up to a week.

Recipe Notes:

Per serving (for 6 servings) Calories 349, Fat 23 g, Carbohydrate 5 g, Fiber 2 g, Sugars 2 g, Protein 34 g

Creamy Garlic Chicken

Dairy-Free, Gluten-Free, Paleo

Prep Time: 10 Mins // Cook Time: 15 Mins

Servings: 2

Yield: 3

Serving Size: 1/3 Recipe

Ingredients

- 3 medium chicken breasts (approx 1.3lbs)
- 1 ¾ teaspoon fine salt, divided
- 1 teaspoon ground cumin
- ½ teaspoon black pepper
- ½ teaspoon mustard powder
- ¼ teaspoon nutmeg
- 2 tablespoons olive oil
- 5 cloves garlic, sliced
- 3 sprigs thyme, leaves only
- 1 lemon
- ½ cup bone broth
- 1 ½ cup cashew cream (see post for nut free)
- 9 ounces spiralized zucchini, 2 medium squash

Instructions

1. Put your chicken breasts on a plate and pat them dry. Then season with 1 ½ teaspoon salt, cumin, pepper, mustard powder, and nutmeg.
2. Pour the 1 tablespoon olive oil in your skillet. Add the chicken and sear without moving for 4 minutes. Flip over, cover the skillet and cook another 3 minutes. Remove the chicken from the skillet and set on a cutting board.

3. Add the remaining oil to the skillet. Add in the garlic and thyme. Sauté until the garlic is toasted and very aromatic. Add in the lemon juice and bone broth, bring to quick simmer. Gently stir to deglaze the skillet.

4. Add in the cashew cream and remaining salt, gently stir as it begins to thicken, 3-4 minutes, then remove from heat. Slice the chicken breasts, and serve one breast with 3 ounces of zoodles on each plate. Cover with ½ a cup of creamy garlic sauce. Enjoy!

5. You can also add the zoodles and sliced chicken back into the skillet and mix it all together before serving, but folks might fight over who got more sauce

CALORIES: 391, FAT: 19.1g, CARBOHYDRATES: 8.8g, FIBER: 2.2g, PROTEIN: 41.1g

Keto Teriyaki Bowl

Dairy-Free, Gluten-Free, AIP, Nut-Free, Paleo

Prep Time: 10 Mins // Cook Time: 35 Mins

Yield: 4

Serving Size: 1/4 of Recipe

Ingredients

MEATBALLS

- 2 pounds ground beef 85%lean
- 1inch nub fresh ginger, peeled and zested
- 1 heaping teaspoon grated citrus zest (I used orange and lime)
- 2 teaspoons garlic powder
- 2 teaspoon fine salt
- 1 teaspoon dried parsley
- 2 tablespoons minced fresh cilantro, more to garnish
- Half a ripe hass avocado

FOR COOKING

- 4 tablespoons avocado oil, more as needed

SAUCE

- 1/3 cup bone broth
- 1 tablespoon fish sauce
- 1 tablespoon red wine vinegar
- ¼ cup coconut aminos, divided
- 1 scoop gelatin

FIXINGS

- 4 cups shredded Brussels sprouts
- 5 cloves garlic sliced
- 4 large eggs

NOODLES

- 4 bags shirataki noodles or veggie noodles like zoodles for Whole30

Instructions

1. Pre-heat oven to 400F.
2. In a large bowl mix together, the ground beef with the rest of the meatball ingredients until well combined, the avocado should be completely mixed in with only traces of green specks in the meat, no chunks left. Shape 12 large meatballs.
3. Bring a small sauce pot full of water to a boil. Put the 4 large eggs, gently in the pot. Boil for 7 minutes, then drain the water and add ice to the eggs, set aside.
4. Toss the Brussels sprouts on a sheet pan with 2 tablespoons avocado oil and 1 teaspoon salt. Spread them out flat over the sheet pan and pop in the oven- middle rack.
5. Heat a large skillet over medium heat. When it comes to temperature add 2 tablespoons of avocado oil to the skillet and brown 6 meatballs at a time, 2 minutes a side, then transfer to a sheet pan. Repeat with the remaining meatballs and then put them in the oven.
6. Add the meatballs to the oven, with the Brussels sprouts, for 10-15 minutes until the sauce and noodles are ready.
7. In the same sauce pot where you boiled the eggs heat the bone broth with the fish sauce, red wine vinegar, and 2 tablespoons coconut aminos. Bring to a boil and reduce for 10 minutes.
8. Add 1 scoop gelatin to the remaining coconut aminos and let it sit until it gels up solid.
9. In the meantime, drain and rinse your noodles and submerge in cool water. Set aside.
10. Heat the skillet where the meatballs were browned and add a little extra avocado oil. Then add in the sliced garlic and fry until golden. Remove from the skillet.

11. Drain the noodles, add to the skillet, sprinkle with salt and sauté in the garlic infused fat for a few minutes while you finish the sauce. They will coat in the fat and get brown and yummy!

12. Remove the bone broth reduction from the heat, scoop in the solid coconut amino-gelatin mass and whisk into broth until smooth and thick. Set aside.

13. Remove the toasty Brussels sprouts and cooked meatballs from the oven.

14. Assemble your bowls.

15. Divide the noodles in between 4 large bowls, then the Brussels sprouts. Add 3 meatballs to each bowl. Garnish with fried garlic, minced cilantro. Peel the eggs and halve them. Add ½ -1 egg to each bowl.

16. Spoon thick teriyaki sauce generously over each bowl and dig in!!

Recipe Notes:

The Macros Include ALL THE MEATBALLS AND ALL THE SAUCE. The recipe is best with 3 meatballs per person. There will be leftover meat and leftover sauce. However, if you divide the entire recipe by 4... the macros are as listed.

CALORIES: 821, FAT: 56g, CARBOHYDRATES: 18g, FIBER: 7.8g, PROTEIN: 53g

SIDE DISH

Creamy Ranch Cauliflower Risotto

Dairy-Free, Gluten-Free, AIP, Nut-Free

Servings: 4

Course: Side dish

This Creamy Ranch Cauliflower Risotto comes together in just minutes, and is an easy dairy free dish you can add to so many meals!

Ingredients

- 1 Tbsp coconut oil
- 12 oz cauliflower rice fresh or frozen
- 1/4 cup coconut milk
- 1 tsp garlic powder
- 1 tsp onion powder
- 1/2 tsp dried chives
- 1/2 tsp dried dill
- salt & pepper to taste
- chopped fresh parsley or chives optional garnish
- 1/4 cup ranch dressing optional

Instructions

1. In a medium saucepan, heat the coconut oil over medium heat until melted. Add the cauliflower rice and sauté for about 3 minutes to get it cooking.
2. Stir in the coconut milk, herbs, and spices, and simmer until the cauliflower is fully cooked and liquid is absorbed, about 5 to 7 more minutes.
3. Drizzle with ranch (if using) and garnish with fresh herbs. Add additional seasonings to taste. Enjoy!

Notes

- Fresh or frozen cauliflower rice will work the same! Frozen may just need a minute or two longer to cook.
- Not a fan of coconut milk? Allergic? You can substitute any milk that works for you. This recipe is really flexible.
- My "Ranch Seasoning" blend in the recipe below is so good on roasted veggies, potatoes, or in an egg bake or scramble! Make extra while you've got the herbs & spices out and store some in a little jar!

Italian Dressing Recipe

Dairy-Free, Gluten-Free, Nut-Free

Prep Time: 4 Mins || Cook Time: 5 Mins

Yield: 16 spoons

Recipe Type: side

An easy zesty Italian vinaigrette—just throw a few ingredients in a jar and shake.

Ingredients

- 1 tablespoon chopped fresh herbs - I used Italian flat leaf parsley
- 1 teaspoon dried oregano
- 1 clove garlic minced with a garlic press
- 1/2 teaspoon sea salt or more to taste
- 1/4 teaspoon fresh cracked black pepper
- 1/4 cup red wine vinegar
- 3/4 cup organic extra virgin olive oil

Instructions

1. Shaking Method: Add all ingredients to a jar or bottle with a tight-fitting lid and shake vigorously until well combined.
2. Whisking Method: Add all ingredients to a mixing bowl and whisk until the ingredients come together.
3. Taste and adjust seasonings if needed.

Calories: 91kcal | Fat: 10g | Saturated Fat: 1g | Sodium: 73mg | Potassium: 2mg | Vitamin A: 50IU | Vitamin C: 0.2mg | Calcium: 4mg | Iron: 0.1mg

Chunky Avocado Salsa Recipe

Dairy-Free, Gluten-Free, AIP, Nut-Free

Prep time: 15 minutes | Cook time: 0 minutes

Yield: 8 servings

Serving size: ½ cup

Ingredients:

- 1 packet (2 tablespoons) Avocado Oil
- 6-8 Roma tomatoes, diced
- ½ red onion, diced
- 1 large jalapeño, finely diced
- 3-4 medium semi-firm avocados, diced
- 2 tablespoons apple cider vinegar
- Juice from 1 lime
- 2 cloves garlic, minced
- 1 teaspoon Kosher salt
- ¼ teaspoon ground black pepper
- Dash of hot sauce

Instructions

- In a large bowl, combine the FBOMB Avocado Oil with the rest of the ingredients.
- Adjust seasoning if needed and serve immediately.

Nutritional Information Per Serving:

Calories: 185 , Fat: 15g, Protein: 2g, Carbs: 10g, Fiber: 6g, Net Carbs: 4g, Macros:, Fat: 73%, Protein: 4%, Carbohydrates: 22%

Roasted Broccoli & Cauliflower with Lemon & Garlic

Dairy-Free, Gluten-Free, AIP

Prep Time: 5 Mins || Cook Time: 35 Mins

Yield: 4-6

Recipe Type: side, Salad

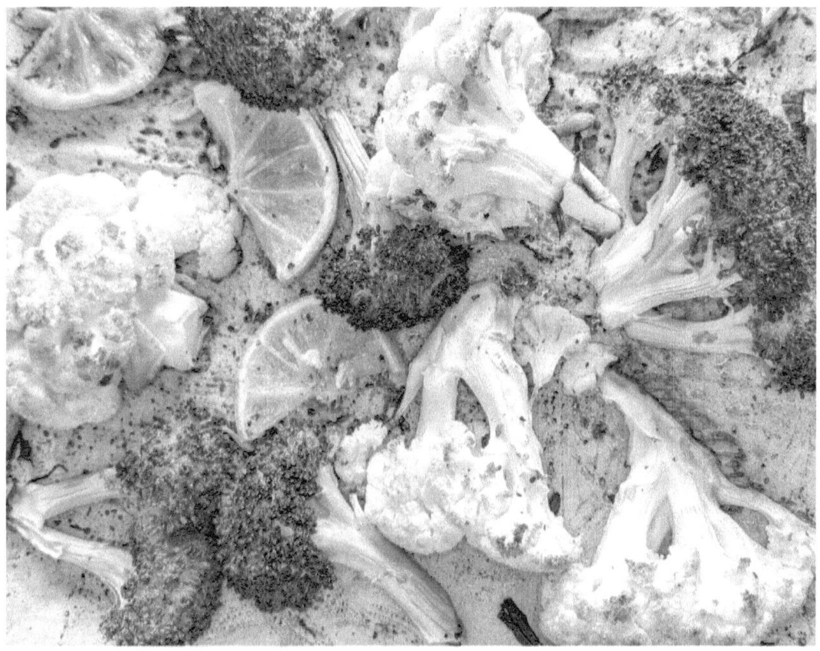

Roasted vegetables are a healthy, easy side dish that can be added to any meal. This vegan-friendly broccoli and cauliflower dish uses just a few simple ingredients but is jam-packed with flavor.

Ingredients

- 1 head of broccoli
- 1/2 head of cauliflower
- 4 garlic cloves
- 1 lemon
- 2 tablespoons olive oil extra virgin
- salt and pepper to taste

Instructions

1. Preheat oven to 425 degrees.

2. Cut broccoli and cauliflower into large florets. Peel and thinly slice garlic cloves. Cut lemon in half and then into thin slices.

3. On a parchment paper-lined baking sheet toss broccoli, cauliflower, garlic cloves and lemon together with extra virgin olive oil. Coat evenly. Season generously with salt and pepper.

4. Roast in preheated oven for 35 minutes or until the floret edges begin to brown and curl.

Remove from the oven and give everything another good toss before serving. Enjoy!

Avocado Cauliflower Rice

Dairy-Free, Gluten-Free, Nut-Free

Serves: 6 cups

Prep Time: 5 mins || Cook Time: 15 mins

Cooking Type: Baking

Course: Side dish

An easy side dish, this Avocado Cauliflower Rice takes riced cauliflower and adds smashed avocado, jalapeño, lime juice, and cilantro for a delicious paleo, Whole food, and low carb dish perfect to pair with just about anything!

Ingredients

- 6 cups cauliflower rice
- 1 tablespoon cooking fat (avocado oil, coconut oil)
- 1 cup diced yellow onion (120 grams)
- 3 cloves garlic, minced
- 2 large avocados, diced (300 grams)
- 1 jalapeño, diced
- 2 1/2 tablespoons lime juice
- 1/2 cup packed cilantro, roughly chopped
- salt and pepper, to taste

Instructions

1. Heat a large sauté pan over medium heat. Add oil and let it get hot. Once hot, add diced onions and sauté for 5 minutes until translucent, stirring occasionally. Add garlic and cook for another minute. Add the cauliflower rice and let cook for 6-7 minutes, stirring occasionally, until softened.
2. While the rice cooks, make the avocado mash. Add avocados, diced jalapeno, lime juice, and salt and pepper to a large bowl and mash with a fork until combined, but a little texture remains.
3. Once cauliflower rice is cooked to your preference, remove from heat. Add avocado mixture to cauliflower rice and mix well to combine. Stir in cilantro. Top more cilantro and jalapeño if desired. Enjoy!

Calories 151 Calories from Fat 90

Total Fat 10g 15%, Saturated Fat 2.6g 13%, Polyunsaturated Fat 0.1g, Monounsaturated Fat 5g, Potassium 715.9mg 20%, Carbohydrates 14g 5%, Dietary Fiber 7.4g 30%, Sugars 5.4g, Protein 4g 8%, Vitamin A 4.6%, Vitamin C 121.9%, Calcium 4.9%, Iron 5.7%

Spaghetti Squash Pizza Nests

Dairy-Free, Gluten-Free, Nut-Free

Serves:12

Prep Time: 10 mins || Cook Time: 1 hr 20 min

Cooking Type: Baking

Course: Side dish

Spaghetti Squash Pizza Nests are tasty, low carb, gluten free, noodle nests with pizza inside.

Ingredients

- 1 medium size spaghetti squash (about 2 1/2 cups squash noodles
- 2/3 cup tomato sauce * try to get one without added sugars
- ½ tsp garlic powder
- 1 ½ tsp Italian seasonings
- ¼ tsp oregano
- Pinch sea salt
- 24 slices pepperoni * I like uncured nitrate free brands
- ½ tbsp chopped basil fresh or lightly dried

Instructions

1. Preheat oven to 400 F (204 C), and line or oil a baking sheet.
2. Using a skewer or knife, poke holes all over the spaghetti squash. Place on baking sheet and bake for an hour, turning over halfway through.
3. Remove squash from oven and cool until cool to touch. Leave oven on 400F (204 C).
4. Grease or oil 2 muffin pans.
5. While squash is cooling, Combine in a medium size mixing bowl: tomato sauce, garlic powder, Italian seasonings, and oregano. Mix together.
6. Once squash is cool, slice in half and using a fork scrape noodles into a large bowl.
7. Place squash noodle mixture into muffin cups and make a well in the center of each with a spoon.
8. Add tomato sauce mixture to each well.
9. Add a pepperoni slice to each well
10. Sprinkle with chopped basil, and bake at 400 F (204 C) for 25 minutes or until set.
11. Serve.

Guacamole Chicken Salad

Dairy-Free, Gluten-Free, Nut-Free

Prep Time: 10 mins || Cook Time: 20 min

Cooking Type: Baking

Serves:3

Course: Side dish

Since guacamole and chicken salad are two of our favorite things, I decided it was time to combine them! This guacamole chicken salad is mayo-free, packed with flavor, protein, and perfect for easy lunches! It's paleo, Whole30 compliant and keto friendly, too.

Ingredients

- 2 avocados medium
- 1/3 cup onion minced
- 2 cloves garlic minced
- 1-2 jalapeno pepper minced (adjust for spice preference)
- 2-3 Tbsp fresh lime juice or to taste
- 2 Tbsp chopped fresh cilantro plus more for garnish
- Sea salt to taste
- 1 lb chicken breast seasoned with salt and pepper and cooked (about 2-2.5 cups cooked)

Instructions

Cook chicken (this step should be done ahead of time so the chicken has time to cool.)

1. Preheat your oven to 400 degrees and line a baking sheet with foil. Drizzle olive oil over chicken and turn to coat.
2. Season on both sides with sea salt, black pepper, plus onion + garlic powder, if desired. Bake in the preheated oven for 20 minutes or until cooked through (no longer pink in the middle and juices run clear.)
3. Allow chicken to cool completely, then either dice or shred depending on what you prefer for chicken salad.

assemble salad:

1. In a large bowl, add the cooked diced chicken with all remaining ingredients except for the salt. Mix well, mashing avocado as you mix.
2. Once fully combined, add sea salt to taste. Serve immediately, leftovers will keep for about a day in the refrigerator but because the avocado will brown, it won't last much longer than that. Enjoy!

Calories: 240kcal Fat: 14g Saturated fat: 2g Cholesterol: 58mg Sodium: 111mg Potassium: 741mg Carbohydrates: 8g Fiber: 5g Sugar: 1g Protein: 21g Vitamin A: 175% Vitamin C: 15.4% Calcium: 19% Iron: 0.8%

Smoked Salmon Cucumber Dill Salad!

Dairy-Free, Gluten-Free

Prep Time: 15 Mins // Cook Time: 35 Mins

Servings: 6

Dinner Ideas that's Keto, Low Carb and Healthy... Delicious of course! Well this here you'd want to have more. You can taste the Zest from the lemons, the Caramelized mushrooms with the smokiness from the Salmon. Yummy!

Ingredients:

- A pack of Wild Smoked Salmon
- 4 English Cucumbers
- Fresh Dill
- Lemon or Lime Zest
- 2 Sliced Avocados
- 1/2 Cup Sliced very thin Green Cabbage
- 1 Cup Fine Sliced Romaine lettuce
- 1 Cup Fine sliced Green Kale
- 1 Cup Fine Slices Mushrooms
- A head of fresh Red Onion
- 5 Cloves of Fresh Garlic
- 1/2 Lemon
- 1/2 Tsp. Salt
- 1/2 Tsp. Garlic powder
- 1/2 Tsp. Onion Powder
- 1 Tbl Oregano
- 1 Tbl Basil

Instructions:

10. In a Pan, Caramelize the Onions, Garlic, Mushrooms with Avocado oil (Don't add too much oil because we are trying to caramelize this and just add a pinch of Salt on Low to Medium heat - Once done just set aside to cool down.
11. Shave the cucumbers and set that aside.
12. Slice up the lettuce, Kale, Cabbage and Avocados and Set that aside.
13. Add you spices or whatever spices you personally prefer in a small bowl and mix well to combine the mixture.
14. Zest the Peel from the Lemon or Lime and set that aside. Get your olive oil ready.
15. Squeeze the 1/2 of one Lemon or Lime, and set that aside.
16. Slice up your smoked Salmon.

17. Once you have prepared everything, Start adding all to a big bowl. (Make sure you mix very carefully).

18. At the end add your olive oil - Add as much as you like, please taste and see you like to add more, but little at a time. Add your fresh dill for Garnish and a strong delicious Aroma taste.

Turnip, Leek, And Greens Hash

Dairy-Free, Gluten-Free, Nut-Free

Prep Time: 30 mins || Cook Time: 15 mins

Serves: 6

Serving size: 1 serving

Ingredients

- 3 cups shredded turnips (from 4 medium size turnips)
- 4 cups shredded kale
- 2 cups shredded leeks
- 2 tbsp balsamic vinegar
- 2 tbsp lard
- 1 tsp sea salt

Instructions

1. Use a food processor with the shredder attachment to shred the turnips and kale.
2. Use a knife to thinly slice the leeks.
3. Heat a large pan with lard on medium-low, and once hot, add in leeks.

4. Stir the leeks around until fragrant, then add in shredded kale and sea salt.
5. Allow the mixture to cook 2-3 minutes, then add in the balsamic vinegar, mixing it around until the vinegar has dissipated.
6. Add in the shredded turnips, stir the mixture around, allowing it to cook until the turnips have just softened and then serve.

RECIPES NOTES

For low-FODMAP, simply use leek greens instead of the white part of the leek

Easy Sardines Salad

Dairy-Free, Gluten-Free, Nut-Free

Prep Time: 5 minutes || Cook Time: 0 minutes

Yield: 1 serving

Category: Salad

Ingredients

- 1 can (4-5 oz. or 120 g) sardines in olive oil or brine, drained
- 1/4 lb (approx. 100 g) salad greens
- 1/10 lb (approx. 50 g) deli meat or bacon or leftover meat, chopped small
- 1 Tablespoon (15 ml) olive oil
- 1 Tablespoon (15 ml) lemon juice
- Salt to taste

Instructions

1. Prepare the salad greens by tossing them in the olive oil and lemon juice.
2. Add the deli meat in and toss.
3. Top with the drained sardines.
4. Sprinkle with salt to taste.

Net Carbs: 1 g, Calories: 400 Sugar: 0 g Fat: 34 g Carbohydrates: 2 g Fiber: 1 g Protein: 30 g

Super Easy Guacamole

Dairy-Free, Gluten-Free, Nut-Free

Prep Time: 5 minutes ||Cook Time: 0 minutes

Yield: 2 servings

Category: Side Dish

Get this super easy and fast Keto guacamole recipe here – it takes just 5 minutes to make. It's Paleo, low-carb, and autoimmune-friendly (AIP).

Ingredients

- 1 ripe avocado, mashed
- 1 Tablespoon garlic powder
- 1/2 Tablespoon onion powder
- 2 teaspoons lime juice
- Salt to taste
- 2 Tablespoons fresh cilantro, finely chopped or use 2 teaspoons of dried cilantro

Instructions

1. Mash up the avocado. Make sure your avocado is ripe as it won't make very good guacamole otherwise.
2. Mix in the garlic powder and onion powder.
3. Squeeze in the fresh lime juice and finely chopped cilantro.
4. Mix everything together really well. Add salt to taste and serve.

Net Carbs: 6 g

Calories: 180 Sugar: 2 g Fat: 15 g Carbohydrates: 13 g Fiber: 7g Protein: 3 g

Roasted Garlic on the Grill

Dairy-Free, Gluten-Free, Nut-Free

Serves: 20 cloves

Prep Time: 2 mins || Cook Time: 30 mins

Course: Side dish

You won't believe how easy this is. With just 3 essential ingredients you have a creamy garlic spread.

Ingredients

- 2 garlic heads
- 2 teaspoons olive oil
- sea salt to taste

Instructions

1. Set up the grill for indirect heat and preheat to 350 - 400 degrees (or preheat oven).
2. Cut the top off of garlic heads, making sure each individual clove has the tip cut off so you can squeeze the garlic out easily once it's roasted.
3. Drizzle with olive oil, sprinkle with sea salt and wrap each garlic head in a double layer of foil.
4. Roast 30 - 45 minutes in a closed grill (or oven), until garlic feels soft when squeezed.

Note: one head of garlic contains about 10 cloves

Calories: 3kcal | Vitamin C: 0.1mg | Calcium: 1mg

Baked Asparagus

Dairy-Free, Gluten-Free, Nut-Free

Prep Time: 15 Mins // Cook Time: 35 Mins

Servings: 6

Recipe Type: side

These are delicious just the way they are. Very healthy and healing for your gut. Asparagus has allot of health benefits and one main it's high in Fiber, High in Vitamins, Nourishes the digestive track and more!

Ingredients:

- 1-2 Bunches Organic Asparagus
- 5-8 Cloves Garlic
- 1 Tsp. Pink Salt
- 1 Tbl Oregano
- 1 Tsp. Onion Powder
- 1 Tsp. Lemon or Lime Zest
- 2 Tbl Avocado Oil or Olive Oil Pure.
- Lemon or Lime Juice - However much you like.

Instructions:

9. Cut off 1 inch of the bottom root of the Asparagus and give it a good wash.
10. Place the Asparagus in the oven Pan, spread out.
11. In a little "Ceramic Mash bowl" place the Garlic with the spices and give it a good "Mash".
12. Add the wet ingredients to the mashed garlic, give it a good stir.
13. Pour onto the Asparagus.
14. Drizzle some Lemon or Lime juice (Which ever you prefer).
15. Bake on 350F for about 20-30 minutes. Don't over Bake (Don't let it discolor) Let there be a crisp to the Asparagus.
16. Enjoy!

Cauliflower Alfredo Sauce

Dairy-Free, Gluten-Free, Nut-Free

Prep Time: 10 mins || Cook Time: 12 mins

Yield: 2 cups

Category: Sauces

The best dairy free alfredo you will ever taste, made from cauliflower, no joke.

Ingredients

- cups cauliflower florets
- cloves garlic, peeled
- 1 cup additive free coconut milk (water and coconut)
- tablespoons lard
- 1 tablespoon Red Boat Fish Sauce
- 1 tablespoon red wine vinegar
- 1 teaspoon fine salt

Instructions

1. Fill a sauce pan with about an inch of water and add the cauliflower and garlic. Heat the pan over medium-high heat and bring to a boil with the lid on.
2. Cook for about 8 minutes, until the cauliflower is fork-tender. Remove from the heat and drain.
3. Place the cauliflower, garlic and remaining ingredients in a blender. Puree until smooth.
4. Store in an airtight container in the fridge for up to 10 days. To reheat, bring to a simmer in a saucepan over medium heat.

Serving Size: 1/2 Cup

Calories: 250, Fat: 24g, Carbohydrates: 9g, Fiber: 3.4g, Protein: 3.5g

Keto Tuna Salad Recipe

Dairy-Free, Gluten-Free, Nut-Free

Prep: 15 min

Serves: 2

Ingredients

- 1 cup cooked tuna, flaked
- 1 celery stalk, minced
- 1/2 cucumber, peeled and diced
- 1 green onion, sliced
- 1/4 cup homemade mayonnaise (Recipe in this cookbook)
- 1 tbsp. fresh lemon juice
- Sea salt

Instructions

1. In a bowl combine the Paleo mayonnaise, lemon juice, and season to taste.
2. In another bowl combine all the other remaining ingredients.
3. Pour the mayo mixture over the tuna and toss until everything is well mixed.
4. Cover and refrigerate until ready to eat.
5. Serve the tuna salad over fresh greens.

Keto Zuppa Toscana Recipe

Dairy-Free, Gluten-Free, Nut-Free

Prep Time: 10 mins || Cook Time: 30 mins

Servings: 2

Ingredients

- 150 g beef mince
- rashers fatty bacon, finely diced
- 2 cups cauliflower florets
- 1 cup sliced kale
- 1 cup coconut milk
- 2 cups chicken broth
- 1 medium onion, finely diced
- 1 teaspoon chopped garlic
- Half a teaspoon dried basil
- Half a teaspoon dried thyme
- A pinch of turmeric
- 2 tablespoons cooking oil of your choice
- Salt to taste

Instructions

1. In a pot or large pan with a lid, at medium heat add onions and fry them until they are golden brown, then add bacon and cook for about 2 minutes until it's cooked, then add the mince.
2. Fry the mince until it loses its raw color and is starting to brown, then add the garlic.
3. Cook for about 2 minutes turning the mince from time to time.
4. Add the basil, thyme, salt and turmeric and cook for a further minute, then take the mince off the pan and set it aside leaving the fat in the pan.
5. Add the cauliflower to the pan, adding more cooking oil if needed and sauté until it starts to loose rawness, for about a minute.
6. Add the kale and cook until it starts to wilt.
7. Add the chicken broth and bring to a simmer and cook for about 2 minutes until the cauliflower is soft.
8. Add the mince back in and add the coconut milk in as well.
9. Taste and season with more salt and herbs if needed.
10. Cover with a lid and lower the heat so it simmers slowly for about 5 minutes before serving.

Fillet

Dairy-Free, Gluten-Free, Nut-Free, Vegan

Prep Time: 10 min || Cook Time: 15 min

Serves 2

Dredged rather than battered, these filets are a lighter-on-the-carbs and grain-free version of classic fried fish.

Ingredients

- to 4 filets Cod, 4-5oz each, set at room temperature for an hour
- 1/4 cup Coconut flour
- 1/4 cup Arrowroot starch
- 1/8 tsp Garlic powder
- 3/4 tsp Himalayan salt, or to taste
- 3/4 cup Avocado oil

Instructions

1. Wash filets under cool water. Shake excess moisture and lay them in a single layer on doubled up kitchen towelsor paper towels.
2. You want to have a little bit of moisture left on them so that the coating sticks. (Dabbing and rubbing a few drops of water on the filets right beforehand also helps!)

3   In medium mixing bowl, stir together flours and seasonings well. Taste a tiny pinch to see if you desire more seasonings.

4   Heat a cast iron skillet or ceramic nonstick pan over medium-high heat. Add avocado oil to pan and allow to come to about 350 F. (You should not really have to measure the temp, as this is shallow frying.

5   Just be sure not to make it too cool or hot. You will know the oil is ready when it gently sizzles when you sprinkle a pinch of your flour mixture into it. If it doesn't sizzle, the oil is too cold. If it burns, then you need to turn the heat down and wait a few minutes to test again.)

6   A splatter screen is very useful here in preventing hot oil spatter burns and messes.

7   Alternately, use a compact electric deep fryer for more accurate and safer food frying.

8   Dredge the filets in the coating, patting the mixture onto the fish a little bit to get it to stick (it can be a little finicky as it's a delicate coating).

9   Gently slide in the filets one at a time, ensuring not to overcrowd the pan. Fry in batches if necessary to keep oil temperature high enough to crisp the fish.

10 Using a silicone fish turner, gently flip the filets over after 4 minutes, and cook another 3 to 4 minutes or until exterior is golden-crisped and fish is cooked through in center. Be careful not to overcook or the fish will become tough and rubbery.

11 Set finished filets on a plate lined with clean doubled-up kitchen or paper towels. This absorbs excess oil and makes for a crispier crust.

Notes

If a thicker coating is desired, whisk together a "gelatin egg" (1 Tb gelatin plus 3 Tb room temperature water), allow to rest for a few minutes, then brush it thinly on the filets just before coating in the flour mixture.

Serve with AIP Tartar Sauce:

1   Mix 1/4 cup of my No-Mess No-Egg Mayo, with 1 to 2 Tb lemon juice, 1 Tb chopped capers (Mediterranean Organic is a good clean brand), and 1 to 2 Tb either chopped up sauerkraut or my Raw & Easy Paleo Pickles.

2   Also, a couple dashes of dried dill and a tsp of dried parsley.

Creamy Cucumber Dressing

Dairy-Free, Gluten-Free, Nut-Free, Vegan

Prep Time: 5 Minutes

Servings: 10

Ingredients

- 1/2 cucumber
- 1/2 cup additive free coconut milk (water and coconut only as ingredients)
- garlic cloves, pressed
- tbsp olive oil
- 1 tbsp lemon juice
- 1/2 tsp salt
- 1-2 tbsp dill, finely chopped

Instructions

1. Remove peel from cucumber.
2. Slice in half lengthwise and remove seeds by scraping a spoon over the seeds making sure not to scrape the flesh.
3. Once seeds are remove, pat cucumber dry with paper towel.
4. Chop the cucumber, should have approximately 1/2 cup.
5. Place cucumber, coconut cream, olive oil, garlic, lemon juice, and salt in a blender.
6. Blend until smooth.
7. Remove dressing from blender and mix in dill.

Enjoy!

Notes

Store in refrigerator for up to 4 days.

Garlic Oregano Olive Tapenade Recipe

Dairy-Free, Gluten-Free, Nut-Free, Vegan

Prep Time: 5 minutes || Cook Time: 0 minutes

Yield: 2 servings

Ingredients

- 1 cup (approx. 5 oz. or 140 g) pitted compliant olives
- 1 Tablespoon fresh oregano leaves
- cloves garlic (add more if you like it really garlicky)
- Tablespoons extra virgin olive oil

To Serve:

- 1–2 zucchini
- cans complaint sardines

Instructions

1. Place all the ingredients into a blender and blend really well.
2. To serve, shred the zucchini and divide between two bowls. Top with the tapenade and sardines.

Calories: 180 Sugar: 0g Fat: 18g Carbohydrates: 5g Fiber: 2g Protein: 1g Cholesterol: 0g

Strawberry Caramelized Onion Vinaigrette

Dairy-Free, Gluten-Free, Nut-Free, Whole30

Prep Time 5 minutes || Cook Time 20 minutes

Ingredients

CARAMELIZED ONION:

- tsp refined olive oil
- 1/2 sweet onion, halved then thinly sliced

VINAIGRETTE:

- 1/4 cup strawberries quartered
- Tb white wine vinegar -or-apple cider vinegar
- 1 Tb honey, optional (for Whole30 and Keto: omit)
- 1 large clove garlic
- 1 to 2 tsp Himalayan salt, or to taste1 tsp onion powder
- 1/4 tsp ginger powder
- 1/2 tsp dried tarragon
- 1/2 tsp dried thyme
- 1 tsp dried parsley
- 1/4 cup extra virgin olive oil
- 1/2 cup refined avocado -or- refined olive oil
- 1 to 4 Tb water to thin, if desired

Instructions

1. Heat a small cast iron skillet over medium heat for 5 minutes. When hot, add oil to melt.
2. Add onions and stir. Cook, stirring occasionally, for about 5 minutes until beginning to brown.
3. Turn heat to low/medium-low and cook for about 10 minutes more, stirring occasionally to prevent scorching. Onions are ready when they are soft, golden, and translucent.
4. Transfer onions to a plate and cool 10 minutes.
5. To a high-speed blender, add onions, strawberries, vinegar, honey (if using), garlic, salt, onion powder, /ginger, herbs and extra virgin olive oil. (You'll use the refined oil in a moment, but not just yet.)
6. Blend on medium-high for 30 seconds or until mixture is very smooth.
7. Keep blender running, then slowly drizzle in the refined oil in a steady stream. Vinaigrette will emulsify and become "creamy."
8. If mixture is too thick to your liking, blend in 1 Tb water at a time until desired consistency.
9. Taste and adjust seasonings, tartness, and sweetness if desired.

10 Store in an air-tight jar up to 2 weeks in the fridge.

11 Contents may settle and separate, so give the jar a good shake before opening.

Notes

1 You may also use an immersion blender instead of a high-speed blender. Simply layer the ingredients in the order listed in a wide-mouth jar.

2 Gently plunge the blender head to the bottom of the jar then turn it on high, keeping the head at the bottom of the jar as it blends.

3 When mixture is starting to appear smooth about half-way up the sides of the jar, begin to slowly pull the blender head up. When you reach the top, plunge a few times to get all the oil to emulsify into the vinaigrette.

Keto Chicken Wings - Crispy Garlic "PAN FRIED"

Dairy-Free, Gluten-Free, Nut-Free, AIP

Prep Time: 10 minutes || Cook Time: 20 minutes

Servings: 4 serves

Calories: 264

Chicken Wings are a great source of fat for your Ketogenic Diet and there are so many ways to prepare them. Our Keto Chicken Wings are just like fried chicken, without needing a deep fryer.

Ingredients

- Chicken Wings
- 1 teaspoon garlic powder
- 1/2 teaspoon Salt
- ounces tallow
- lemon wedges to serve

Instructions

1. Separate the wings, keeping the drumettes and the middle section. Discard the tip (you'll now have 20 pieces)
2. In a mixing bowl, marinate the chicken wings in the garlic powder, salt and allow to sit aside for 15 minutes.
3. Add the tallow to a large non-stick frying pan and heat over medium to high heat.
4. When the tallow has melted and is very hot, add the wing pieces and fry for 5 minutes.
5. Turn the wing pieces over, place a lid on the pan and fry for another 5 minutes.
6. Remove the lid and turn the wing pieces, cook without the lid for a further 5 minutes. Depending on the size of the wing pieces, they will be ready.
7. To check if they are ready you can cut though one of the larger pieces and check if the flesh is cooked, or use a meat thermometer and ensure the temperature is above 70C/160F.
8. Remove from the pan. Serve with lemon wedges.

Serving: 5pieces | Calories: 264kcal | Carbohydrates: 0.4g | Protein: 21g | Fat: 20g | Saturated Fat: 7g | Polyunsaturated Fat: 3g | Monounsaturated Fat: 8g | Cholesterol: 73mg | Sodium: 561mg | Potassium: 154mg | Vitamin A: 150IU | Calcium: 0.1mg | Iron: 0.9mg

APPETIZER

kale and blueberry salad recipe

Dairy-Free, Gluten-Free, Nut-Free, AIP, Vegan

Prep Time: 5 mins || Cook Time: 0 minutes

Yield: 2 servings

Category: Appetizer

Serving Size: 1 plate

Ingredients

- 6 oz. (170 g) kale, chopped roughly
- 10 blueberries
- 1 Tablespoon (4 g) coconut flakes
- 1/4 red onion, cut into thin slices
- 1 Tablespoon (2 g) parsley
- 1 Tablespoon (15 ml) lemon juice
- 2 Tablespoons (30 ml) olive oil
- Salt to taste

Instructions

1   Toss all the ingredients together.
2   Divide between 2 plates and serve.

Net Carbs: 9 g

Calories: 191 Sugar: 2 g Fat: 16 g Carbohydrates: 13 g Fiber: 4 g Protein: 4 g

Keto Lemon Garlic Salmon with Leek Asparagus Ginger Saute

Dairy-Free, Gluten-Free, Nut-Free, AIP

Prep Time: 10 minutes || Cook Time: 20 minutes

Yield: 2 servings

Ingredients

For the lemon garlic salmon:

- filets of salmon (with skin on), fresh or frozen (340 g), defrost if frozen
- 1 Tablespoon (15 ml) avocado oil
- cloves garlic (12 g), minced
- teaspoons (10 ml) lemon juice
- Salt to taste
- Lemon slices to serve with

For the leek asparagus ginger sauté:

- spears of asparagus (160 g), chopped into small pieces
- 1 leek (90 g), chopped into small pieces
- teaspoons (4 g) ginger powder (or use finely diced fresh ginger if you have it available)
- Avocado oil or olive oil to sauté with
- 1 Tablespoon lemon juice
- Salt to taste

Instructions

1. Preheat oven to 400 F (200 C).
2. Place each salmon filet on a piece of aluminum foil or parchment paper.
3. Divide the oil, lemon juice, minced garlic between the two filets – place these on top of the salmon. Sprinkle with some salt. Then wrap up the salmon in the foil and place into the oven.
4. Open up the foil after 10 minutes in the oven and then bake for another 10 minutes.
5. While the salmon is cooking, place 1-2 tablespoons of avocado oil or olive oil into a frying pan and sauté the chopped asparagus and leek on high heat. Saute for 10 minutes and then add in the ginger powder, lemon juice, and salt to taste. Saute for 1 more minute.
6. Serve by dividing the sauté between 2 plates and placing a salmon filet on top of each.

Net Carbs: 11 g

Serving Size: 1 plate Calories: 680 Sugar: 4 g Fat: 51 g Carbohydrates: 15 g Fiber: 4 g Protein: 43 g

Cauliflower Dip

Dairy-Free, Gluten-Free, Nut-Free, AIP, Vegan

Prep Time: 10 minutes ||Cook Time: 30 minutes

Yield: 2 servings

Category: Appetizer

Ingredients

- 1/2 head of cauliflower (300 g), broken into florets
- 3 Tablespoons of olive oil (45 ml), divided
- 3 cloves of garlic (9 g), unpeeled
- 2 Tablespoons of lemon juice (30 ml)
- Sea salt, to taste
- Radishes and cucumber sticks, to serve with

Instructions

1. Preheat the oven to 400°F (200°C).
2. Place cauliflower florets in a bowl and toss with 2 tablespoons of olive oil.
3. Spread them out on a greased baking tray.
4. Take the garlic cloves as they are and secure inside a small foil parcel where no air can escape. Place onto the same tray.

5. Roast in the oven for 30 minutes, tossing the cauliflower after 15 minutes to ensure even roasting.
6. Remove the roasted, caramelized cauliflower florets (which should have completely softened) and put into a mini food processor.
7. Carefully open the garlic foil parcel and squeeze the roasted flesh from the skins into the same processor. Add the lemon juice (check for pips) and the additional tablespoon olive oil and blitz the mixture to a smooth puree. Season with salt to your liking.
8. Serve the roasted cauliflower dip with fresh, washed radishes and cucumber sticks, or any other vegetables you may prefer.

Calories: 225 Sugar: 5 g Fat: 21 g Carbohydrates: 10 g Fiber: 4 g Protein: 3 g

Creamy Cucumber Salad

Dairy-Free, Gluten-Free, Nut-Free, AIP, Vegan

Prep Time: 5 minutes || Cook Time: 0 minutes

Yield: 2 servings

Category: Appetizer

Ingredients

- 1 cucumber (220 g), sliced and then quartered
- 2 Tablespoons of coconut cream (30 ml)
- 2 Tablespoons of lemon juice (30 ml)
- Salt, to taste

Instructions

1. To make the creamy cucumber salad, mix together (in a small bowl) the cucumber slices, coconut cream, and lemon juice.
2. Add salt to taste.

NOTES

All nutritional data are estimated and based on per serving amounts.

NUTRITION

Calories: 116 Sugar: 1 g Fat: 12 g Carbohydrates: 2 g Fiber: 1 g Protein: 1 g

Lemony Prosciutto-Wrapped Asparagus

Dairy-Free, Gluten-Free, Nut-Free, AIP, Vegan

Prep Time: 10 Mins // Cook Time: 15 Mins

Yield: 4

Recipe Type: Dessert

A quick and easy side dish or appetizer that is Whole30, paleo, and Keto friendly!

Ingredients

- 16 pieces asparagus ends trimmed
- 8 pieces prosciutto
- 1 lemon
- olive oil or avocado oil spray

Instructions

1. Preheat oven to 450. Line a baking sheet with foil or parchment paper.
2. Cut all of the prosciutto pieces in half. Wrap one half around each piece of asparagus, tucking the ends underneath to hold in place.
3. Place the wrapped asparagus pieces on the baking sheet, making sure to leave some room in between each piece.

4. Spray the pieces of asparagus with oil (lightly). Cut your lemon in half, and squeeze one half over all of the asparagus.
5. Slice the other half into rounds and place them on top of the asparagus. Bake for 12 mins. Enjoy!

One-Bowl Keto Blueberry Muffins
Dairy-Free, Gluten-Free, Nut-Free, AIP

Serves: 12 muffins

Prep Time: 10 mins || Cook Time: 20 min

Cooking Type: Baking

Course: Dessert

These keto blueberry muffins have a crisp top and a soft, fluffy inside! They have a sweet nutty flavor thanks to almond butter and almond flour, and are loaded with plenty of juicy sweet blueberries. They're paleo, gluten-free, dairy-free, and low carb.

Ingredients

- 3 eggs room temp
- 1/2 cup smooth almond butter (a drippier one is best for this recipe)
- 2 Tbsp dairy-free milk almond or coconut
- 1/2 cup erythritol
- 2 tsp pure vanilla extract
- 1 Tbsp lemon juice
- 1 1/4 cups blanched almond flour
- 3/4 tsp baking soda
- 1/4 tsp sea salt
- 1 cup blueberries divided

Instructions

1. Preheat your oven to 325 and line a 12 cup muffin pan with parchment liners.
2. In a large mixing bowl, whisk together the eggs, almond butter, milk, erythritol, vanilla, and lemon juice.
3. Add in the almond flour, baking soda, and salt and mix well with a spatula or spoon, don't over-mix.
4. Fold in 2/3 of the blueberries, then spoon batter into muffin liners to make 12 muffins. Add remaining blueberries to the top of the batter.
5. Bake in the preheated oven for 18-20 minutes or until tops are browning and a toothpick inserted near the center of one comes out clean. Allow to cool in pan for 5 minutes, then transfer to wire racks to cool completely.
6. Once cooled, serve or store loosely covered at room temperature for up to two days, or refrigerate or freeze to keep longer.

Calories: 156kcalFat: 12gSaturated fat: 1gCholesterol: 40mgSodium: 144mgPotassium: 106mgCarbohydrates: 6gFiber: 2gSugar: 2gProtein: 6gVitamin A: 75%Vitamin C: 1.9%Calcium: 70%Iron: 1%

Roasted Cauliflower Hummus

Dairy-Free, Gluten-Free, Nut-Free, AIP, Vegan

Serves: 6

Prep Time: 15 mins || Cook Time: 30 min

Cooking Type: Roasting

Course: Appetizer

This cauliflower hummus recipe is a perfect blend of tahini, lemon, and garlic.

Ingredients

- 1 head cauliflower cut into florets
- 1/3 cup extra virgin olive oil divided
- 1/3 cup tahini
- 1 clove garlic peeled
- juice of 2 lemons
- 1/2 - 1 teaspoon sea salt to taste

Instructions

1. Preheat oven to 425 degrees.
2. Toss cauliflower florets with 1 tablespoon olive oil and a pinch of salt. Roast on a rimmed baking sheet until fork tender and caramelized, about 20 minutes. Cool completely.
3. Add roasted cauliflower, tahini, garlic, lemon juice, salt, and olive oil to food processor. Process until mixture reaches hummus consistency. Taste and adjust seasonings. Add water, if needed, to thin.

Calories: 211kcal | Carbohydrates: 8g | Protein: 4g | Fat: 19g | Saturated Fat: 2g | Cholesterol: 0mg | Sodium: 33mg | Potassium: 358mg | Fiber: 2g | Sugar: 2g | Vitamin A: 10IU | Vitamin C: 50.7mg | Calcium: 40mg | Iron: 1.1mg

Grilled Eggplant and Roasted Red Pepper Dip

Dairy-Free, Gluten-Free, Nut-Free, AIP, Vegan

Serves: 6

Prep Time: 10 mins || Cook Time: 45 min

Cooking Type: Baking

Course: Appetizer

Serving size: 1 ½ cups

Grilled eggplant, roasted red pepper, and grill-roasted garlic star in this Italian inspired dip.

Ingredients

- 1 large eggplant
- 1 head garlic
- 1/2 cup diced roasted red peppers
- tablespoons olive oil plus more for drizzling
- tablespoons lemon juice
- 1 tablespoon chopped fresh basil plus more for garnish
- sea salt and fresh ground pepper to taste

Instructions

1. Preheat grill to 400 degrees.
2. Slice top off of garlic, drizzle with olive oil, and sprinkle with sea salt. Wrap in foil and place on grill over indirect heat. Roast until garlic is soft and caramelized, 30 - 45 minutes.
3. Place eggplant on grill and roast with lid closed, turning occasionally, until eggplant is soft, 30 - 45 minutes.
4. Cut eggplant in half and place in colander to drain and cool. Set garlic aside to cool.
5. Peel and dice eggplant. Mash 4 cloves of roasted garlic. Combine eggplant, mashed garlic, peppers, 3 tablespoons olive oil, lemon juice, basil, salt, and pepper. Taste and adjust seasonings.
6. Garnish with an extra drizzle of olive and fresh basil.

Calories: 91kcal | Carbohydrates: 6g | Protein: 1g | Fat: 7g | Saturated Fat: 1g | Cholesterol: 0mg | Sodium: 162mg | Potassium: 210mg | Fiber: 2g | Sugar: 2g | Vitamin A: 95IU | Vitamin C: 10.5mg | Calcium: 20mg | Iron: 0.4mg

Deviled Eggs with Bacon and Chives

Dairy-Free, Gluten-Free, Nut-Free, AIP, Vegan

Serves: 6

Prep Time: 15 mins || Cook Time: 15 mins

Course: Appetizer

Deviled eggs are a quick snack or easy appetizer. This simple recipe is a perfect base for bacon, chives, roasted red peppers, and olives.

Ingredients

- 6 hard-boiled eggs
- 1 tablespoon whole grain Dijon mustard
- 1 tablespoon olive oil
- 1 teaspoon garlic infused olive oil
- 1 - 2 teaspoons lemon juice
- sea salt & pepper to taste

Toppings

- 2 tablespoons crumbled cooked bacon
- 2 tablespoons snipped chives
- 2 tablespoons sliced olives
- 2 tablespoons chopped roasted red peppers

Instructions

1. Peel eggs and slice in half lengthwise. Place egg whites on serving tray and add egg yolks to mixing bowl.
2. Add mustard, olive oils, lemon juice, salt and pepper to egg yolks. Mash with fork until creamy. If needed, add water to thin, one teaspoon at a time. Taste and adjust seasonings.
3. Fill egg whites with yolk mixture and top generously with desired toppings.

Calories: 131kcal | Carbohydrates: 1g | Protein: 7g | Fat: 10g | Saturated Fat: 2g | Cholesterol: 189mg | Sodium: 232mg | Potassium: 79mg | Fiber: 0g | Sugar: 0g | Vitamin A: 340IU | Vitamin C: 3.4mg | Calcium: 27mg | Iron: 0.7mg

Roasted Garlic Baba Ganoush

Dairy-Free, Gluten-Free, Nut-Free, AIP, Vegan

Prep Time: 10 mins || Cook Time: 45 min

Serves: 8

Cooking Type: Baking

Course: Appetizers

An easy dip recipe that is gluten-free and paleo-friendly made with the traditional ingredients.

Ingredients

- 1 head garlic
- 2 medium eggplant
- 3- 4 tablespoons lemon juice juice of 1-1/2 to 2 lemons
- 2 tablespoons tahini
- 2 tablespoons extra virgin olive oil plus more for drizzling
- ½ teaspoon sea salt

Instructions

1. Preheat oven to 400 degrees.
2. Cut the top off the head of garlic. Place on a sheet of foil and drizzle with olive oil. Wrap tightly in foil and place on a rimmed baking sheet with the eggplants.
3. Roast the vegetables for about 45 minutes, until the eggplants are collapsed and the garlic is completely soft.
4. Cut the eggplants in half lengthwise and place in a colander to cool and drain. Open the garlic packet to cool.
5. Peel the eggplants and squeeze the flesh from the garlic head. Place all ingredients in the food processor and pulse to desired consistency. Taste and adjust seasonings.

Calories: 88kcal | Carbohydrates: 9g | Protein: 2g | Fat: 5g | Saturated Fat: 0g | Cholesterol: 0mg | Sodium: 149mg | Potassium: 300mg | Fiber: 3g | Sugar: 4g | Vitamin A: 25IU | Vitamin C: 6.3mg | Calcium: 22mg | Iron: 0.5mg

Cilantro Lime Dressing

Dairy-Free, Gluten-Free, Nut-Free, AIP, Vegan

Prep Time: 5 Minutes

Servings Serving Size: 2 Tablespoons

Yield: 8

Five minute, thick and creamy Avocado Cilantro Lime Dressing - fresh, zesty and packs a punch! Use for topping off salads and dipping veggies.

Ingredients

- 1 bunch fresh cilantro | about 2 cups packed - stems and all*
- 2 large cloves |1 heaping tablespoon garlic
- 3 tablespoons | 45 ml lime juice
- 6 tablespoons | 90 ml extra virgin olive oil
- 1/2 teaspoon salt
- 1/2 teaspoon red chili flakes
- 1 avocado
- 1-2 tablespoons water (optional)

Instructions

1. Add all of the ingredients to a blender and blend until smooth. Taste and season with more salt and lime juice as you see fit.

NOTES

- Make sure to wash and dry your cilantro well before using.
- Keep store in the fridge for up to a week

Amount Per Serving: Calories: 122 Total Fat: 13g Saturated Fat: 2g Sodium: 149mg Carbohydrates: 2g Fiber: 1g Sugar: 0g Protein: 0g

FOR AIP: Use honey or maple syrup as your sweetener of choice

Avocado and Lime Agua Fresca

Dairy-Free, Gluten-Free, Nut-Free, AIP, Vegan

Ingredients

- 1 large ripe avocado
- 1/2 cup fresh lime juice
- 1/3 cup granulated Swerve (or) monk fruit
- 4 cups cold water
- Ice for serving

Instructions

1. In a blender, blend together the first 4 ingredients until smooth.
2. Pour over ice and serve.

Feel free to start with 1/4 cup of sweetener and adjust the sweetness according to your own personal preference.

For AIP: Use honey in place of the sugar alcohol